500

cocktails

500
cocktails

the only cocktail compendium you'll ever need

Wendy Sweetser

SELLERS
PUBLISHING

A Quintet Book

Published by Sellers Publishing, Inc.
161 John Roberts Rd., South Portland, ME 04106
For ordering information:
(800) 625-3386 Toll Free
(207) 772-6814 Fax
Visit our Web site: www.sellerspublishing.com
E-mail: rsp@rsvp.com

ISBN: 978-1-4162-0521-0
Library of Congress Control Number: 2008900988
QTT.COCT

This book was conceived, designed, and produced by
Quintet Publishing Limited
6 Blundell Street
London N7 9BH
United Kingdom

Project Editor: Ben Hubbard
Designer: Susi Martin
Art Director: Sofia Henry
Photography: Ian Garlick
Food Stylist: Wendy Sweetser
Managing Editor: Donna Gregory
Publisher: James Tavendale

10 9 8 7 6 5

Manufactured in Singapore by Pica Digital Pte Ltd.
Printed in China by Toppan Leefung Printers Ltd.

contents

introduction

No one can say for certain where the word "cocktail" came from or who mixed the first one. Back in 1806, certain sections of American society were already condemning "a vulgar but stimulating bittered-sling made of spirits, sugar and water," and there was a range of commercially produced mixes on sale — presumably aimed at those less upright members of the community not averse to the occasional display of vulgarity in their own homes.

The first book of recipes for making cocktails was published in 1862. *Entitled How to Mix Drinks or The Bon-Vivant's Companion*, it was written by a famous bartender of the day called Jerry "The Professor" Thomas and became a best seller. The Jazz Age introduced these "stirred and shaken" phenomena to the wider world, and many stories speculating on how they came to be known as "cocktails" date from this time. Most involve cockfighting, pretty young girls, and gallant, heroic men, but another contender is a French-born New Orleans chemist, Antoine Amedee Peychaud. The creator of his own range of bitters, Monsieur Peychaud offered tipples in eggcups to visitors at his Pharmacie Peychaud drugstore. The drinks became known as coquetiers (French for eggcups), and legend has it that it was only a matter of time before the word became Americanized as "cocktails."

The cocktail's popularity grew rapidly during the 1920s, when the arrival of Prohibition tested the bartender's skill to the limits. He had to search for novel ways to turn bootleggers' bathtub gin or "moonshine" (which was undrinkable neat) into something more palatable to keep his clients happy, and the answer was to disguise it with anything and everything that came to hand. No longer were bars the sole preserve of world-weary men. Now wives and girlfriends began accompanying them to the backstreet speakeasies, where the entrance was by a coded knock on the door and cocktails became the drink of the day. The more outlandish and suggestive cocktail names became, the more customers loved them, seduced by their aura of decadence and illicit glamor.

Three-quarters of the classic cocktails ordered in bars today — including the Martini, the Daiquiri, and the Mint Julep — were created before the start of the twentieth century, but it was Prohibition that ensured their immortality. By 1929 more than 120 recipes for making a Martini were in circulation. Bartenders reluctant to break the law found themselves out of work. Many crossed the Atlantic to open new establishments in Europe, and customers who could afford it followed them. Harry's New York Bar in Paris and the American Bar at the Savoy hotel in London — both still going strong today — were just two of many serving wealthy Americans with drinks they could enjoy in public.

In the early years, cocktails tended to be short and strong, with alcohol as the main ingredient. Customers demanded a quick hit and preferred not to sit looking at the same glass for too long. Today the opposite is more likely to be true. Most cocktails are long and cool, with the alcohol diluted with plenty of fruit juice or mineral water, and the whole thing enjoyed as a pleasant way to unwind.

During the twentieth century, many bartenders became as legendary as their celebrity clientele. Among the most famous were Giuseppe Cipriani, who created the Bellini (champagne and fresh peach juice) at Harry's Bar in Venice, and Johnny Brooks, reputed to mix the driest Martinis in town at New York's Stork Club for starry customers such as Ernest Hemingway and Marlene Dietrich. Another was Don Beach, who, at his Beachcomber restaurant in Hollywood, served Zombies (a potent blend of three types of rum, apricot brandy, and fruit juice) and sixty-two other exotic tipples to the film capital's elite.

Ice, fresh fruit juice, bitters, a slug (or three) of liquor, and the world's most beautiful people have always added up to a seductively heady brew. If you're a cocktail novice who wants to learn more, the recipes in this book will not only help get you started but also show you how to improvise, experiment, and create your own cocktails as well. You'll run out of occasions to celebrate long before you've exhausted new ways to stir, shake, muddle, and mix the ultimate party drink.

stocking the bar

With so many spirits on the market and new ones appearing all the time, deciding on the essentials for creating a reasonably stocked bar can be a challenge. Storage space and financial considerations will limit the aspirations of most fledgling bartenders, but once you've acquired the basics, these can be added to as you go along. The good news is that, unlike table wine, opened bottles of spirits and liqueurs have a long shelf life, so the contents don't have to be finished immediately.

The following list is a varied selection of alcoholic drinks to get you started, plus the most popular mixers and extra items you'll need.

spirits
Gin
Whiskey (Scotch or Irish)
Vodka
Dark and light rum
Brandy or Cognac
Tequila
Dry and sweet vermouth
Bourbon
Triple Sec or Cointreau

liqueurs
A selection of liqueurs according to personal preference, such as Tia Maria, Amaretto, Apricot (or another fruit) Brandy, Crème de Menthe, Drambuie, Blue Curacao, Apple (or another flavored) Schnapps, Advocaat.

wines
Red wine
Dry white wine
Champagne or another sparkling wine such as Cava

mixers
Sparkling mineral water and/or soda water
Tonic water
Dry ginger ale
Cola
Lemonade
Coconut milk
Grenadine and other syrups
Tomato juice and fresh fruit juices, including unsweetened lemon and lime
Angostura bitters
Tabasco or another hot sauce
Worcestershire sauce

sweeteners

Cocktails can be sweetened with the addition of blended or muddled fresh fruit and freshly squeezed juices, or by adding sugar in the form of cubes, superfine sugar, or a syrup. In cooler climates fruit is often less sweet and fragrant than in the tropics, so if you find the cocktail you've made with mango, pineapple, or another exotic fruit isn't as sweet as you'd like, adjust the flavor by adding a couple of dashes of syrup until the balance is right.

Sugar syrup is the easy way to sweeten a drink. Sugar doesn't dissolve easily in alcohol, so using syrup means there are no gritty granules left at the bottom of the glass. Nonalcoholic, ready-made syrups are available at gourmet or liquor stores, or on the internet. These include "gomme" (plain cane-sugar syrup), orgeat (almond flavored syrup), plus dozens of flavored syrups that add their own color and flavor, from grenadine (pomegranate), passion fruit, and cassis (black currant) to the more esoteric violet, vanilla, chocolate, and lavender.

basic sugar syrup

It's easy to make your own sugar syrup.

2 cups granulated sugar
1 cup (8 fl. oz.) cold water

Put granulated sugar in a heavy-based saucepan, add cold water, and let stand for 5 minutes to give the sugar crystals time to absorb the water and soften. Place over a low heat, stirring occasionally until the sugar has completely dissolved and the liquid is clear. Bring to the boil, then lower the heat again, and simmer for 1 minute. Remove the pan from the stove, skim any scum from the surface of the syrup, and leave to cool. Pour into jars, cover, and store.

the finishing touches

Slices or wedges of fresh fruit — apple, pineapple, orange, lemon, lime, kiwi, mango, melon
Fresh whole berries — strawberries, raspberries, blackberries
Maraschino cherries
Cucumber slices or sticks
Celery stalks with leaves
Spices — nutmeg, cinnamon, ginger
Olives
Fresh mint sprigs
Strips of citrus zest

And don't forget, you'll need lots and lots and lots of ice, both cubes and crushed. Freeze lemon and lime wedges, fresh herb leaves, and small edible flowers in ice cubes for a decorative effect.

equipment

Screw-top jars, ordinary kitchen spoons, wooden rolling pins, or pestles, measuring spoons or cups, and a cooler packed with ice, can all double as shakers, stirrers, muddlers, jiggers, and ice buckets, but if you plan to become a serious cocktail maker, it's worth investing in proper, good-quality equipment.

jigger
A spirit measure, usually with a cup at each end. The smaller cup holds a single shot of 1 fl. oz. (equivalent to 2 tablespoons), the larger a double shot of 2 fl. oz. (4 tablespoons). Get comfortable with using a jigger when making cocktails, even if you're measuring less than 1 fl. oz. Soon you'll use it with as much ease as a measuring spoon or cup.

bar spoon
A long-handled spoon, made of stainless steel, with a fairly flat bowl. Used for stirring drinks and for pouring one spirit on top of another when making layered cocktails.

muddler
A wooden, pestle-like tool used to mash or squash fresh fruit and herbs together in the bottom of a glass or shaker to release their aroma and flavor.

shaker
Two basic types of cocktail shaker are available. The standard model is made of stainless steel and generally consists of three components: a canister for holding ice, a tight-fitting lid with a built-in strainer, and a twist-off cap. The Boston shaker usually comes in two pieces: a mixing glass as the base and a stainless steep top. A strainer — such as the popular hawthorn strainer — is needed to filter the cocktail from this type of shaker into a glass. A shaker may be glamorous, but a jam jar with a tight-fitting screw-top lid will work equally well.

electric blender

A real timesaver for making crushed ice. A heavy-duty blender or food processor with robust blades and a powerful motor is needed to crush ice cubes, otherwise break them up first by placing them in a strong plastic bag and bashing with a hammer or rolling pin. To extend the life of the blades, process the fruit or other ingredients before adding the ice.

measuring cup

A large measuring cup is useful for mixing large quantities of cocktails. Make up batches and keep in sealed jars or bottles in the fridge. Shake well before serving.

ice cube bags

These take up less room in the freezer than ice cube trays. You can pull out just the number of cubes you need rather than having to empty the whole tray.

ice bucket

Essential for storing ice cubes. Use tongs or a small scoop to dispense the ice — never your hands. Not only is it unhealthy — frozen fingers are agony!

kitchen basics

A small serrated knife, vegetable peeler (for shaving off strips of zest), chopping board, citrus press or basic lemon squeezer, cloth to wipe up spills, serving tray, and coasters are all useful to have at hand when preparing and serving cocktails.

decorations & accessories

Don't overload glasses with too many stirrers, straws, paper parasols, tropical flowers, exotic fruit slices, or colored toothpicks — with cocktails, less is definitely more.

the right glass

Each type of cocktail has its own special shape of glass, but as long as you follow a few basic rules, it's not necessary to invest in all the different styles.

Shot glasses are small, straight-sided, and used for single measures of spirit, that are drunk neat. Short drinks served "on the rocks" need plain, squat tumblers known as shorts, sours, or old-fashioned glasses. Those with solid glass studs covering the base are designed for slammers and therefore tougher than standard tumblers, as they must survive being banged sharply on the table top before the drink inside is tossed down.

Tall, straight highball glasses and the slightly deeper collins glasses are for long, mixed drinks, while the iconic Martini glass is stemmed with a wide, triangular bowl. When simply a cocktail glass is specified in a recipe, any small, stemmed glass that is wide at the top can be used, including a Martini glass.

Saucer-shaped champagne glasses might look spectacular stacked high for a sparkling wine pyramid fountain, but their lack of depth means the bubbles in the wine disappear almost as soon as it is poured. For champagne cocktails or any others made with sparkling wine, tall-stemmed flutes are best because they trap the bubbles in the glass for longer. Any cocktail served without ice should be poured into a stemmed glass so the drinker's hand doesn't warm the cool mix inside.

Creamy piña coladas and other blended drinks — particularly those from the Caribbean islands — are often served in stemmed goblets or tulip-shaped glasses, while large-bowled brandy balloons allow plenty of leeway for swirling and inhaling the spirit's aroma. When choosing glasses, one with a fine rim is generally more pleasant to drink from than a thick-edged, heavy glass, and a long, slender stem sits more comfortably in the hand.

preparing glasses

Always chill glasses in the freezer for half an hour (no longer or they might crack) or in the refrigerator for an hour. To frost a glass, bury it in crushed ice or leave it in the fridge until very cold. When serving long, mixed drinks, fill highball glasses half to three-quarters full with ice cubes before pouring in the drink. Never reuse ice; it must be fresh every time.

salting or sugaring the rim

Rub the rim of the glass with a wedge of lemon or lime, and dip the rim in fine salt or superfine sugar, depending on the cocktail you are making.

different glasses (as pictured opposite)

Top Row	Bottom Row
1 low-stemmed highball glass	1 old-fashioned tumbler
2 low-stemmed highball glass	2 Collins glass
3 champagne flute	3 sherry glass
4 goblet	4 highball glass
5 champagne flute	5 stemmed cocktail glass
6 large tulip-shaped glass	6 white wine glass
7 margarita glass	7 Martini glass
8 sekt glass	8 brandy balloon
9 small tulip-shaped glass	9 old-fashioned glass
10 lager glass	10 bowl-shaped stemmed cocktail glass
11 Martini glass	11 shorts glass

terms & techniques

stirring

Put ice cubes into a mixing glass, add the ingredients, and stir everything together for about 10 seconds until the alcohol is chilled but not diluted by the ice. Strain or pour directly into a serving glass, leaving the ice behind.

shaking

Put crushed ice in a cocktail shaker until half-filled, add the cocktail ingredients (which should not include any sparkling wine or carbonated drink), cover with the lid, and shake vigorously up and down for about 10 seconds until the shaker has frosted on the outside. Strain into a chilled serving glass.

mixing

Put the cocktail ingredients in a blender and blend quickly to mix or reduce to a smooth purée, topping off with extra juice or mineral water if too thick. If your blender has a heavy-duty motor, ice cubes can be used; otherwise use crushed ice.

flairing

If you see yourself as the next Tom Cruise and fancy emulating his bottle-flipping/tossing/spinning expertise, as he demonstrated in the film *Cocktail*, there are plenty of bar schools and academies on the Internet who offer "flairing" courses. Much better than trying to teach yourself and watching all those precious bottles crash to the floor!

muddling

Mash fresh fruit and herbs to a smooth paste using a special muddling tool, the back of a spoon, a pestle, or small rolling pin. This can be done in a cocktail shaker or directly in the serving glass.

floating

When making layered cocktails, each spirit or liqueur needs to be added slowly and carefully by being poured gently into a glass over the back of a spoon, in the same way as cream is floated on top of an Irish coffee. As density levels vary from spirit to spirit, it is important to add them in the order given in a recipe so each floats on top of the one below without sinking. You can work out density levels yourself by checking each bottle for its percentage of alcohol. The higher the percentage, the less dense it is, and the higher it will layer in a glass. The lower the percentage, the lower it will layer. A layered cocktail is served with the layers still separate, not stirred together.

tips & tricks of the trade

• Get all your ingredients and equipment ready before you start making a cocktail. If you're having a party and it isn't practical to leave the cocktail making until guests arrive, prepare mixes ahead and keep them chilled, ready to shake, stir, or blend when needed.

• Serve a cocktail as soon as it's poured into a glass, as it will separate on standing.

• Avoid overloading cocktail shakers, blenders, or pitchers. Don't fill glasses to the brim or they'll overflow.

• Always tell guests what a cocktail contains — fix labels to pitchers or punchbowls if your guests are serving themselves — and make sure there are nonalcoholic alternatives for drivers and nondrinkers.

and finally...
Cocktails are sophisticated, sexy, and fun, but however innocent they might taste, they pack a highly intoxicating punch. Drink wisely and don't over-indulge — you'll only regret it.

long, tall classics

Tall and refreshing, these classic highball cocktails

are just the pick-me-up you need after a long day.

From the invigorating Sea Breeze and limpid Blue

Lagoon to the stunning Tequila Sunrise and potent

Long Island Iced Tea, you'll find the perfect cocktail

to suit every mood.

tom collins

see variations page 48

This famous cocktail's history goes back to London in the early 1800s. John Collins, the head waiter at Limmer's Hotel and Coffee House in Mayfair, mixed a popular drink using Dutch Genever gin, but his sling failed to catch on in the United States until a bartender made it with Old Tom Gin, a London gin with a sweet flavor more suited to American tastes. A version of the cocktail — the John Collins — is made with bourbon or whiskey.

2 fl. oz. gin
1 fl. oz. freshly squeezed lemon juice
1 tbsp. sugar syrup
Ice cubes
Soda water
Lemon slice, to decorate

Put the gin, lemon juice, and sugar syrup in a tall glass, three-quarters filled with ice cubes, and top off with soda water. Stir, decorate the glass with a slice of lemon, and a stirrer.

Serves 1

harvey wallbanger

see variations page 49

Everyone agrees that world-champion mixologist Donato "Duke" Antone created this killer cocktail in the 1950s at his Blackwatch Bar in Hollywood. However, the story that he actually made the first one for a California surfer called Harvey, who, wanting to drown his sorrows after suffering a wipeout in a competition, collided with the wall as he tried to leave, is probably the stuff of legend. A less colorful explanation suggests the cocktail's name was inspired by the sight of the tall, leggy Galliano bottles wobbling and banging against the wall as nimble-fingered barmen slid them back behind the bar.

Ice cubes
2 fl. oz. vodka
1/2 cup (4 fl. oz.) freshly squeezed orange juice
1 fl. oz. Galliano
Orange wedge, to garnish

Half-fill a tall glass with ice cubes. Pour in the vodka and orange juice, stir well, and then float the Galliano on top, carefully pouring it over the back of a bar spoon. Serve with a stirrer and straw. Hook an orange wedge over the side of the glass. Before drinking, squeeze orange into the cocktail and drop it into the glass.

Serves 1

raffles singapore sling

see variations page 50

The recipe for this world-famous sling, which was created around 1915 by Ngiam Tong Boon, the bartender of the Raffles Hotel in Singapore, and served in the Long Bar to luminaries such as Somerset Maughan, Noel Coward, and film star Douglas Fairbanks, was mislaid long ago. The modern mix probably bears little resemblance to the original, but it's still a hit with tourists and high-flying executives, who pack into the Long Bar to sip the legendary cocktail. In time-honored fashion, customers toss the shells of the monkey nuts served with their drinks onto the floor. The sound of the shells crunching underfoot echoes the sound made by feet walking over the dried leaves that were scattered on the floors of the old plantation houses.

Ice cubes
1 fl. oz. gin
3/4 fl. oz. cherry brandy
1/2 fl. oz. Cointreau
1/2 fl. oz. Benedictine
1/2 fl. oz. freshly squeezed lime juice

2 fl. oz. pineapple juice
3 fl. oz. freshly squeezed orange juice
Dash of Grenadine
Dash of Angostura bitters
Slice of pineapple and a maraschino cherry,
  to decorate

Put half a dozen ice cubes in a cocktail shaker and pour in the gin, cherry brandy, Cointreau, Benedictine, fruit juices, Grenadine, and Angostura. Shake and strain into a tall glass. Decorate with a slice of pineapple and a maraschino cherry. Serve with a stirrer and a straw.

Serves 1

blue lagoon

see variations page 51

When Blue Curacao first appeared in the 1960s, cocktail drinkers were quickly seduced by the cool, lagoon-like concoctions appearing in their glasses. This blend of vodka, Blue Curacao, and lemonade was the creation of Andy McElhone, son of the legendary Harry of Harry's New York Bar, although his original recipe was made with lemon juice rather than lemonade.

Crushed ice
1 fl. oz. vodka
1 fl. oz. Blue Curacao
1/2 cup (4 fl. oz.) lemonade
Lime wedge, to decorate

Half-fill a tall glass with crushed ice. Pour in the vodka and Blue Curacao and top off with the lemonade. Decorate glass with a wedge of lime.

Serves 1

cape codder

see variations page 52

A popular long drink named after the summer playground along the Massachusetts coast. One thing's for certain — there can't be many nicer ways to unwind than sitting at your oceanside cotttage, watching the sun set over the Atlantic, and slowly sipping a cool Cape Codder.

Ice cubes
2 fl. oz. vodka
5 fl. oz. cranberry juice
Lemon or lime wedge, to decorate

Half fill a tall glass with ice cubes and add the vodka and cranberry juice. Stir well and serve with a lemon or lime wedge dropped in the drink or tucked over the edge of the glass. Add a stirrer and straw.

Serves 1

cuba libre

see variations page 53

Probably the most famous rum cocktail in the world, the first Cuba Libres were reputedly drunk in 1900 to toast both the island's newly won independence and the arrival of the latest must-have soft drink — Coca-Cola.

Ice cubes or crushed ice
2 fl. oz. white rum
5 fl. oz. cola
1 lime

Half fill a tall glass with ice cubes or crushed ice. Add the rum and top off with the cola. Cut the lime in half and squeeze half into the glass. Cut the remainder of the lime into small wedges and add them to the glass. Serve with a stirrer and straw.

Serves 1

long island iced tea

see variations page 54

Not quite as innocent as it might sound, this is a hit-the-spot mix of four or five white spirits. Many variations using different spirit combinations exist, some leaving out the tequila, others the vodka, but however you mix it, it's still liquid relaxation in a glass.

Ice cubes
1/2 fl. oz. white rum
1/2 fl. oz. gin
1/2 fl. oz. vodka
1/2 fl. oz. tequila
1/2 fl. oz. Cointreau or Triple Sec
1 tbsp. fresh lime juice
Cola (to taste)
Lime and orange zest, to decorate

Half-fill a tall glass with ice cubes, the size of the glass being determined by how strong you want the finished drink. Add the rum, gin, vodka, tequila, Cointreau or Triple Sec, and lime juice. Top off with cola, making the drink as strong or as diluted as you wish. Decorate glass with lime and orange zest.

Serves 1

sea breeze

see variations page 55

This long, cool cocktail dates from the 1930s, when it was made with gin instead of vodka, plus apricot brandy and lemon juice, with a splash of Grenadine to provide a feminine pink hue. In 1980s California, the popularity of the grapefruit diet with the local girls led to grapefruit juice replacing the apricot brandy and cranberry juice the Grenadine.

2 fl. oz. vodka
3 fl. oz. cranberry juice
3 fl. oz. grapefruit juice
Crushed ice

Pour the vodka, cranberry juice, and grapefruit juice into a tall glass half-filled with crushed ice. Serve with a stirrer and stir well before drinking.

Serves 1

horse's neck

see variations page 56

Originally the Horse's Neck was a nonalcoholic concoction of ginger ale, ice, and lemon zest. It was around 1910 that serious drinkers decided the smooth and silky beverage needed a good kick, and added bourbon. Other spirits have been experimented with over the years, but today the most popular ingredient is brandy.

Dash of Angostura bitters
Ice cubes
2 fl. oz. brandy
5 fl. oz. ginger ale
1 lemon

Add a good dash of Angostura to a tall glass and swirl to lightly coat the inside. Half-fill the glass with ice, add the brandy, and top off with the ginger ale. Cut around a lemon with a potato peeler or sharp knife to remove the zest in a long, thin spiral. Hang the zest over the side of the glass — ideally it should stretch right to the base.

Serves 1

tequila sunrise

see variations page 57

This 1930s Mexican mix of tequila and orange juice might have inspired a hit song for the Eagles and a blockbuster movie for Mel Gibson, but for cocktail lovers everywhere it will always be a colorful re-creation of the blazing sun rising over the parched Mexican desert.

Ice cubes
2 fl. oz. tequila
3/4 cup (6 fl. oz.) freshly squeezed orange juice
Generous dash of Grenadine
Orange slice and fresh cherry, to decorate

Put 4 or 5 ice cubes in a tall glass and add the tequila and orange juice. Add a good splash of Grenadine and wait for it to sink to the bottom of the glass. Decorate with an orange slice and a fresh cherry, and serve with a straw and a stirrer.

Serves 1

moscow mule

see variations page 58

Jack Morgan owned the Cock 'n' Bull saloon in Los Angeles during the 1940s. He despaired of his customers ever getting a taste for the ginger beer he'd stockpiled in his cellar until John Martin, the West Coast PR supremo for Smirnoff vodka, walked into his bar one night. Together they devised a new cocktail they christened the Moscow Mule. Although it was traditionally served in a small copper mug, modern bartenders usually find a tall highball glass more practical — and more attractive.

Ice cubes
2 fl. oz. vodka
Juice of 1 lime
5 fl. oz. ginger beer
Lime slices and mint sprigs, to decorate

Half-fill a tall glass with ice cubes. Add the vodka and lime juice and top off with the ginger beer. Serve decorated with lime slices and mint sprigs.

Serves 1

screwdriver

see variations page 59

Long and cool, this elegant cocktail is a comparative newcomer to the bar scene. It was reputedly invented by an American oilman working in Iran in the 1950s who, lacking the appropriate long-handled spoon, stirred his sundowner with a screwdriver from his toolbox. Squeeze in the juice straight from the orange for the freshest and most concentrated flavor.

1 1/2 fl. oz. vodka
Crushed ice
1/2 cup (4 fl. oz.) freshly squeezed orange juice
Orange slice or wedge, to decorate

Pour the vodka into a highball glass three-quarters filled with crushed ice. Gradually add the orange juice, stirring until combined. Serve with a stirrer and decorate the glass with an orange slice or wedge.

Serves 1

tom collins

see base recipe page 27

john collins
Replace the gin with bourbon or whiskey and replace the lemon slice with an orange slice.

jean-paul collins
Replace the gin with French brandy and replace the lemon slice with a maraschino cherry.

caribbean collins
Replace the gin with white rum and replace the lemon slice with a lime slice.

moscow collins
Replace the gin with vodka and replace the lemon slice with a strawberry.

acapulco collins
Replace the gin with tequila and replace the lemon slice with a lime wedge.

variations

harvey wallbanger

see base recipe page 28

long, tall wallbanger
Pour 1 fl. oz. vodka and a dash of Galliano into a tall glass half-filled with crushed ice and top off with freshly squeezed orange juice.

lime mandarin wallbanger
Replace the orange juice with mandarin orange juice and the orange wedge with a wedge of lime.

bison wallbanger
Rather than sticking with plain vodka, experiment by using a flavored vodka such as Bison with its grassy hints of lavender and herbs. Try different flavored vodkas — there are many available, including Toffee, Melon, Coconut.

stiletto
Replace the orange juice with the pulp of 4 passion fruit, which has to be warmed gently to separate the pulp from the seeds and strained. Mix with 1 tablespoon of peach, passion fruit, or nectarine juice, and pour into the glass with the vodka. Decorate with a wedge of passion fruit.

salty dog
Prepare the basic recipe but replace the orange juice with 2 fl. oz. grapefruit juice and pour the cocktail into a glass with a salt-crusted rim.

variations

raffles singapore sling

see base recipe page 31

citrus sling
Replace the pineapple juice with grapefruit juice and use blood or blush-orange juice. Omit the Grenadine and add 1 teaspoon of sugar syrup. Serve with just a cherry.

long bar sling
Instead of making the basic recipe, shake together half a dozen ice cubes with 2 fl. oz. gin, 1/2 fl. oz. Benedictine, 1 fl. oz. cherry brandy, and the juice of 1 orange. Strain into a tall glass and top off with soda water.

cherry gin sling
For an even simpler but equally refreshing sling, pour 2 fl. oz. gin and 1 fl. oz. cherry brandy into a tall glass half-filled with ice cubes. Top off with soda water and decorate with a maraschino cherry.

straits sling
Instead of making the basic recipe, shake together 1 fl. oz. gin, 1/2 fl. oz. each of cherry brandy and Benedictine, 1 teaspoon orange bitters, and the juice of 1/2 lemon. Top off with soda water.

vodka sling
Replace the gin with vodka, adding a double measure if you want a kick.

blue lagoon

see base recipe page 32

pineapple lagoon
Pour the vodka into a tall glass over crushed ice, add 1/2 cup fresh pineapple juice instead of lemonade, and stir well. Float the Blue Curacao on top.

eve's lagoon
Replace the lemonade with sparkling apple juice.

grape lagoon
Replace the lemonade with white grape juice or dry white wine.

sunrise over the lagoon
Add a dash of Grenadine and wait for it to sink to the bottom of the glass before drinking.

sleepy lagoon
Replace the vodka with gin or tequila.

variations

cape codder

see base recipe page 35

rum codder
Replace the vodka with white rum and add a squeeze of lime juice.

gin codder
Replace the vodka with gin and serve with a twist of orange instead of a lemon or lime wedge.

lemon codder
Replace the plain vodka with lemon vodka and serve with a twist of lemon.

tequila codder
Replace the vodka with tequila and serve with orange and lemon slices tucked over the edge of the glass.

bourbon codder
Replace the vodka with bourbon and serve with a lemon wedge and a maraschino cherry.

cuba libre

see base recipe page 36

sundowner libre
Replace the white rum with dark or gold rum and the lime with an orange wedge.

amaretto libre
Replace half the rum with Amaretto Disaronno liqueur.

tequila libre
Replace the rum with tequila and serve with a lemon wedge.

comfort libre
Replace the rum with Southern Comfort and squeeze in the juice from one quarter of an orange.

low-cal libre
Halve the rum amount and increase the quantity of cola to 3/4 cup (6 fl. oz.) but using diet cola.

variations

long island iced tea

see base recipe page 38

lemon tea
Top off with Bitter Lemon rather than cola and drop a slice of lemon into the drink.

mint green tea
Replace the Cointreau with green Crème de Menthe. Decorate with a sprig of fresh mint.

long cool iced tea
Omit the tequila, gin, and Cointreau. Pour the rum and vodka into a tall glass over crushed ice rather than cubes and stir in the lime juice with 1 teaspoon sugar syrup. Top off with cola and decorate with a lime wedge.

apple tea
Top off with sparkling apple juice rather than cola. Instead of lime and orange zest, drop a couple of apple slices into the drink.

russian tea
Omit the rum and gin and increase the quantity of vodka to 1 1/2 fl. oz. using lemon vodka instead of plain. Decorate with a lemon wedge instead of lime and orange zest.

variations

sea breeze

see base recipe page 39

deep purple breeze
Add a splash of Blue Curacao to the glass and stir it in.

virgin breeze
Omit the vodka and increase the amounts of cranberry juice and grapefruit juice to 4 fl. oz. Add a squeeze of lime juice.

thirties breeze
Replace the grapefruit juice with 2 fl. oz. apricot brandy and a good squeeze of lemon juice. Replace the cranberry juice, if you wish, with a splash of Grenadine.

hawaiian breeze
Replace the grapefruit juice with pineapple juice, and the cranberry juice with orange juice. Add a splash of Grenadine and a twist of lime.

cool breeze
Reduce the vodka to 1 fl. oz. and replace the grapefruit juice with soda water.

variations

horse's neck

see base recipe page 41

on the hoof
Replace the brandy with gin and replace the lemon zest with a spiral of orange zest.

bourbon racing cert
Replace the brandy with bourbon. Decorate glass with a spiral of lemon or lime zest.

old nag
Replace the Angostura with 2 or 3 dashes of orange bitters.

italian thoroughbred
Replace the brandy with 1 fl. oz. grappa and 1/2 fl. oz. each of sweet red vermouth and dry white vermouth. Pour the spirits over ice and top off with the ginger ale.

champion hurdler
Replace half the ginger ale with orange juice and decorate the glass with an orange wedge.

variations

tequila sunrise

see base recipe page 42

tequila sun-light
For a lighter drink, mix 2 fl. oz. orange juice with 1 fl. oz. tequila and strain into a glass. Add a dash of Grenadine and wait for it to sink to the bottom.

mexican sunrise
Replace the orange juice with pineapple juice.

strawberry sunrise
Instead of making the basic recipe, pour 1 fl. oz. tequila and 1 1/2 fl. oz. strawberry liqueur into a tall glass over 4 or 5 ice cubes and top off with orange juice. Wait for the strawberry liqueur to sink to the bottom, and serve decorated with an orange slice and a fresh strawberry. Serve with a straw and a stirrer.

blue-day haze
Half-fill a tall glass with ice cubes; add 1 fl. oz. Blue Curacao and 1 fl. oz. tequila; and top off with soda water. The blue Curacao will settle at the bottom of the glass.

soda sunrise
Replace half the orange juice with soda water to give the drink a light spritz.

variations

moscow mule

see base recipe page 45

orange bitters mule
Add a couple of dashes of orange bitters instead of a lime. Decorate with an orange slice.

gingered apple mule
Replace half the ginger beer with still or sparkling apple juice. Instead of the lemon zest, drop 2 or 3 thin apple wedges into the drink.

highland mule
Replace the vodka with Scotch whiskey and the lime juice with the juice of half an orange. Replace the lime slices and mint sprigs with a twist of orange and a maraschino cherry.

brandy mule
Replace the vodka with brandy and the lime juice with 1 tablespoon of lemon juice. Replace the lime slices with a lemon wedge.

stubborn mule
Replace the ginger beer with ginger ale. Replace the lime slices with an orange wedge.

variations

screwdriver

see base recipe page 46

sparkling screw
Replace the ordinary vodka with one of the new sparkling vodkas or, for a less alcoholic tipple, use half vodka and half sparkling mineral water.

comfortable screw
Replace the vodka with Southern Comfort and add a maraschino cherry to the glass.

slow comfortable screw against the wall
Reduce the amount of vodka to 1/2 fl. oz. and add the same quantity of sloe gin and Southern Comfort. Top off glass with orange juice and float a little Galliano on top to make the "wall."

ghostly screw
Celebrating Halloween? Then spook your guests with genuine "black" vodka — not the clear spirit distilled from black Russian potatoes but the one colored with catechu, a herb native to Africa and southern Asia.

scarlet screw
Replace ordinary orange juice with freshly squeezed blood orange juice.

chic & cool

Served in frosted glasses with long stems, these
"short" drinks tell you all you need to know about
how the word "cocktail" became synonymous with
sophistication and intrigue. Many were created or
inspired by the legendary bartenders of the '20s,
'30s, and '40s, and they are just as popular today.

between the sheets

see variations page 82

In the heady days of 1930s America, bartenders vied with each other to keep their customers coming back for more by creating cocktails with more and more seductive names. This sexy mix was an instant success and remains just as popular today.

1 fl. oz. white rum
1 fl. oz. brandy
1 fl. oz. Cointreau or Triple Sec
1 fl. oz. lemon juice
Twist of lemon zest

Put the rum, brandy, Cointreau or Triple Sec, and lemon juice in a cocktail shaker, and shake vigorously. Strain into a chilled cocktail glass and serve decorated with a twist of lemon zest.

Serves 1

stinger

see variations page 83

Before the days of Prohibition, this relaxing pick-me-up was served straight up, but gradually more and more customers began requesting it served on the rocks in a sours or an old-fashioned glass. Which way is best? You choose!

1 1/2 fl. oz. brandy
3/4 fl. oz. white Crème de Menthe

Stir the brandy and Crème de Menthe together and pour into a well-chilled cocktail glass. Serve with a stirrer.

Serves 1

negroni

see variations page 84

In the early twentieth century, Count Camillo Negroni, a Florentine nobleman and a regular in the city's Casoni Bar, wanted a change from his usual Americano cocktail, so he ordered it spiked with a little gin. Happy to oblige a valued customer, the bartender promptly created the perfect predinner drink — a mellow harmony of bitter and sweet that's guaranteed to stimulate the appetite.

Ice cubes
1 fl. oz. Campari
1 fl. oz. sweet red vermouth
1 fl. oz. gin
Twist of orange, to decorate

Half-fill a cocktail shaker with ice; add the Campari, sweet vermouth, and gin; and shake well. Strain into a well-chilled cocktail glass and serve with a twist of orange.

Serves 1

cosmopolitan

see variations page 85

The Cosmo, as it is affectionately known, is definitely one for the ladies, in particular those four sassy New Yorkers from *Sex and the City*. Bartender Cheryl Cook takes the credit for inventing the Cosmopolitan in the 1980s at her South Beach bar in Florida, but a similar drink was popular before that during the late 1970s at San Francisco's gay bars. However, it was only when Toby Cecchini began serving Cosmopolitans at his Odeon bar in New York in the 1990s that it became the iconic cocktail it is today.

Ice cubes
1 1/2 fl. oz. vodka
1 fl. oz. Triple Sec
1 fl. oz. cranberry juice
1 fl. oz. freshly squeezed lime juice
Wedge of lime, to decorate

Half-fill a cocktail shaker with ice cubes and add the vodka, Triple Sec, cranberry juice, and lime juice. Shake and strain into a well-chilled martini glass. Tuck a wedge of lime over the side of the glass and serve.

Serves 1

gimlet

see variations page 86

Back in the days when both spirits and beers were stored in wooden barrels, bartenders used a small, sharp tool called a gimlet to tap into them. This inspired the creation of this short, citrusy cocktail. In 1953 Raymond Chandler added to the gimlet's popularity by making it a favorite tipple of his legendary private eye, Philip Marlowe, in *The Long Goodbye*.

1 1/2 fl. oz. gin
1 1/2 fl. oz. lime cordial
Cracked ice cubes
Small lime wedge, to decorate

Put the gin, lime cordial (such as Rose's Lime Juice, or mix equal parts sugar syrup and fresh lime juice), and 4 or 5 cracked ice cubes into a cocktail shaker, and shake vigorously. Strain into a well-chilled cocktail glass and serve decorated with a small wedge of lime.

Serves 1

manhattan

see variations page 87

Nobody can say for sure when and where this celebrated cocktail was created, but one theory harks back to 1846 when a Maryland bartender mixed while trying to revive a customer who had been injured in a duel. Another points to Winston Churchill's mother, Jenny Jerome, who in 1874 reputedly asked the Manhattan Club in New York City to invent a cocktail for a banquet she was hosting in honor of Governor Samuel J. Tilden. However, as historians have since pointed out, when the event was supposedly taking place, Jenny was far away in England giving birth to her famous son.

2 fl. oz. whisky
1 fl. oz. sweet red vermouth
1 dash of Angostura bitters
Ice cubes
Maraschino cherry, to decorate

Pour the whiskey, vermouth, and bitters into a mixing glass; add 4 or 5 ice cubes; and stir well. Strain into a well-chilled cocktail glass and serve with a maraschino cherry.

Serves 1

lemon drop

see variations page 88

Sharp and sweet, this cool lemon classic is guaranteed to turn a quiet evening into something special. Sugar the rim of the glass and chill well before pouring in the seductive citrus mix.

Lemon wedge
Superfine sugar
Ice cubes
1/2 fl. oz. vodka
1/2 fl. oz. Limoncello
1/2 fl. oz. freshly squeezed lemon juice
Lemon slice, to serve

Rub the rim of a cocktail glass with the lemon wedge. Dip the rim in superfine sugar and chill well. Half-fill a cocktail shaker with ice cubes; add the vodka, Limoncello, and lemon juice; and shake vigorously. Strain into the glass and serve decorated with a lemon slice.

Serves 1

sidecar

see variations page 89

Here's another classic reputedly created at the end of World War I by legendary barman, Harry McElhone, for one of the regulars who frequented his New York Bar in Paris. The customer, an army captain, always arrived at the bar riding in the sidecar of a motorbike driven by his chauffeur.

Ice cubes
2 fl. oz. brandy
1 fl. oz. Cointreau
1 fl. oz. freshly-squeezed lemon juice
Twist of orange, to serve

Half-fill a cocktail shaker with ice cubes and pour in the brandy, Cointreau, and lemon juice. Shake hard and strain into a well-chilled cocktail glass. Decorate with a twist of orange.

Serves 1

daiquiri

see variations page 90

The classic daiquiri of rum, lime, and sugar was dreamed up around 1900 during a hot Cuban summer when Jennings Cox, an American mining engineer who was working on the island, added fresh lime juice and sugar to the local rum because his gin supplies had run out. With important guests to entertain, he christened the mix "daiquiri" after a town near Santiago on Cuba's southeast tip.

2 fl. oz. white rum
2 tbsp. freshly squeezed lime juice
1 tsp. superfine sugar or sugar syrup
Ice cubes
Twist of lime zest, to decorate

Put the rum, lime juice, sugar or syrup, and plenty of ice cubes into a cocktail shaker, and shake vigorously. Strain into a chilled glass and serve decorated with a twist of lime zest.

Serves 1

white lady

see variations page 91

This drink was first shaken and strained by bartender Harry McElhone during his tenure at Ciro's Club off London's Haymarket in 1919, one of the favorite A-list hangouts of its day. The contrast of sweet Cointreau with sharp citrus makes this the perfect aperitif.

Ice cubes
2 fl. oz. gin
1 fl. oz. freshly squeezed lemon juice
1 fl. oz. Cointreau
Wedge or twist of lemon, to serve

Put half a dozen ice cubes in a cocktail shaker; add the gin, lemon juice, and Cointreau; and shake vigorously. Strain into a well-chilled cocktail glass and serve with a wedge or twist of lemon.

Serves 1

grasshopper

see variations page 92

Crème de Menthe turns this creamy treat a cool shade of green, but it's important to use white Crème de Cacao as brown Crème de Cacao will turn it into a dark and muddy pool — although the drink will taste just as good! A light sprinkle of grated chocolate dusted over the surface makes a pretty garnish.

Ice cubes
1 fl. oz. white Crème de Cacao
1 fl. oz. green Crème de Menthe
1 fl. oz. light cream
Grated chocolate, to decorate

Put half a dozen ice cubes in a cocktail shaker; add the Crème de Cacao, Crème de Menthe, and cream; and shake well. Strain into a well-chilled cocktail glass and dust the surface with a little grated chocolate.

Serves 1

golden cadillac

see variations page 93

White Crème de Cacao shaken with Galliano and cream gives this cocktail a gorgeous golden hue. It also makes a slightly sweeter drink than if the more familiar brown Crème de Cacao is used.

1 fl. oz. white Crème de Cacao
1 fl. oz. Galliano
1 fl. oz. light cream
Ice cubes

Pour the Crème de Cacao, Galliano, and cream into a cocktail shaker; add 4 or 5 ice cubes; and shake well. Strain into a cocktail glass.

Serves 1

variations

between the sheets

see base recipe page 61

early night
Replace the white rum with dark rum and replace the lemon twist with a twist of orange.

under the covers
Replace the Cointreau with Blue Curacao and the lemon twist with a maraschino cherry.

mexican sleepover
Replace the rum with tequila.

starry night
Replace the brandy with plain or lemon vodka.

variations

stinger

see base recipe page 62

stinger on the rocks
Pour the brandy and Crème de Menthe mixture together into a tumbler
half-filled with cracked ice cubes.

bourbon stinger
Replace the brandy with bourbon. Serve straight up or on the rocks.

tequila stinger
Replace the brandy with tequila. Serve straight up or on the rocks.

vodka stinger
Replace the brandy with vodka and the white Crème de Menthe with green.
Serve straight up or on the rocks.

variations

negroni

see base recipe page 65

highball negroni
Turn this into a long drink for a hot summer's day by pouring the Campari, vermouth, and gin into a highball glass half-filled with ice and top it off with soda water.

gin and it
Omit the Campari and increase the quantities of vermouth and gin to 1 1/2 fl. oz. each.

rum negroni
Replace the gin with white rum.

vodka negroni
Replace the gin with vodka for a Russian-style Negroni.

cosmopolitan

see base recipe page 66

south beach cosmopolitan
To recreate Cheryl Cook's original Cosmopolitan, substitute lemon vodka for the plain vodka, and add just a splash of Triple Sec, 1 teaspoon lime cordial (such as Rose's Lime Juice), and enough cranberry juice to turn the drink a pretty pink.

cranberry apple cosmo
Replace the lime juice with apple juice, squeeze in the juice from the small wedge of lime, and decorate the drink with a thin, curly strip of green apple peel.

razzamattaz cosmo
Replace the plain vodka with raspberry vodka.

fiery acapulco cosmo
Prepare the basic recipe, but replace the vodka with tequila. Add 2–3 drops of Tabasco to the martini glass and swirl to coat the sides. Strain in the drink and float a small red chili in the drink.

gimlet

see base recipe page 69

gimlet on the rocks
Pour the gin and lime cordial into a sours or old-fashioned glass filled with ice. Stir well and drop a wedge of lime into the glass. Serve with a stirrer.

vodka gimlet
Replace the gin with vodka, and serve straight up or over ice.

tequila gimlet
Replace the gin with tequila, and serve straight up or over ice.

scotch gimlet
Replace the gin with Scotch whiskey.

variations

manhattan

see base recipe page 70

dry manhattan
Replace the whiskey with bourbon and the sweet red vermouth with Noilly Prat Dry Vermouth. Serve with a twist of lemon instead of a maraschino cherry.

not-so-dry manhattan
Make the Dry Manhattan, but add a dash of sugar syrup or 1/2 teaspoon of syrup from the maraschino cherry jar to the mixing glass to sweeten the mix.

sweet manhattan
Omit the Angostura and use equal quantities of whiskey and sweet red vermouth.

west side story
Replace the whiskey with bourbon and half the sweet vermouth with dry vermouth. Serve with a twist of orange and a maraschino cherry.

variations

lemon drop

see base recipe page 72

citrus drop
Replace the Limoncello with Triple Sec.

sweet lemon drop
Double the amount of vodka and omit the Limoncello. Drop a sugar cube
into the glass before pouring in the drink.

melon drop
Replace the Limoncello with Midori melon liqueur and the lemon slice with
a maraschino cherry.

lemon soda drop
Instead of using a tall-stemmed glass, put the ingredients in a highball glass
and top off with cream soda or lemonade.

variations

sidecar

see base recipe page 73

scotch sidecar
Replace the brandy with Scotch whiskey and the orange twist with a twist of lemon.

gin sidecar
Replace the brandy with gin and the Cointreau with Grand Marnier. Replace the orange twist with a halved slice of orange.

vodka orange sidecar
Replace the brandy with lemon vodka and the lemon juice with orange juice. Add a lemon twist to the orange twist.

tequila sidecar
Replace the brandy with tequila and the orange twist with a maraschino cherry.

variations

daiquiri

see base recipe page 75

daiquiri sunrise
Add 2 tablespoons Grenadine syrup to the drink and wait for it to sink to the bottom, or shake the Grenadine with the other ingredients.

minted lychee daiquiri
Reduce the quantity of rum to 1 fl. oz., and add 1 fl. oz. lychee liqueur. Replace the twist of lime zest with a small sprig of mint, floated on top of the drink.

mango daiquiri
Follow the directions for the minted lychee daiquiri, but replace the lychee liqueur with mango liqueur and float a wafer-thin slice of fresh mango on top instead of the mint.

banana daiquiri
Replace half the rum with Crème de Banane, and decorate the side of the glass with a lime slice and a banana slice.

variations

white lady

see base recipe page 76

blue lady
Replace half the Cointreau with Blue Curacao. Serve with a fresh blueberry on a cocktail stick, instead of the lemon twist.

pink lady
Add a splash of Grenadine to the shaker with the other ingredients. Serve with a fresh raspberry on a cocktail stick instead of the lemon twist.

shady lady
Replace the gin with mandarin or pineapple vodka.

wicked lady
Replace the lemon juice with lime juice and add 2 dashes of orange bitters. Decorate the glass with a lime twist.

variations

grasshopper

see base recipe page 79

leaping grasshopper
Replace the light cream with 1 fl. oz. vodka.

mocha hopper
Replace the Crème de Menthe with Kahlúa or Tia Maria.

amarula grasshopper
Replace the light cream with the same quantity of Amarula Cream Liqueur, distilled from South Africa's lush, sweet Marula fruit.

banana hopper
Replace the Crème de Menthe with Crème de Banane.

variations

golden cadillac

see base recipe page 80

amber cadillac
Use brown Crème de Cacao instead of white, and decorate glass with a slice of golden kiwifruit.

pink cadillac
Add a splash of Grenadine to the shaker with the other ingredients.

stretched limo
Pour the shaken drink into a tall glass half-filled with ice and top off with soda water.

orange cadillac
Reduce the quantity of Galliano to 1/2 fl. oz. and add 1 fl. oz. freshly squeezed orange juice.

the marvelous martini

Mythical and mysterious, the Martini reigns

supreme as the world's No. 1 cocktail. Straight up

with a twist, shaken with sweet cherry brandy, or so

dry it'll give the Sahara a run for its money, when it

comes to the world's favorite cocktail, there really is

no contest.

strawberry martini

see variations page 106

A gorgeous, strawberry-pink confection that's sweet, smooth, and fruity. It's definitely one for the girls. Make the drink in summer when fresh strawberries are at their most luscious and fragrant; freeze any extra stawberry purée for another time.

3–4 strawberries, hulled, plus 1 extra to serve
2 fl. oz. vodka
1/2 fl. oz. Crème de Fraise or Crème de Framboise
Juice of 1/2 lime, plus a twist to serve
Ice cubes

Purée the strawberries in a blender or push them through a coarse metal sieve, keeping the extra one whole to decorate the drink. Place 1 tsp. of the purée in a cocktail shaker and add the vodka, Crème de Fraise or Crème de Framboise, lime juice, and plenty of ice cubes. Shake well, strain into a cocktail glass, and decorate the side of the glass with a whole strawberry and twist of lime.

Serves 1

classic martini

see variations page 107

The true origins of the Martini are as clouded by myth and mystery as all other legends. Did this iconic cocktail evolve from an 1862 drink called a "Martinez," a sweet blend of gin, bitters, and red vermouth? Should Martini di Arma di Taggia, the barman at the Knickerbocker Hotel in New York, take the credit with his 1911 mix of gin, white vermouth, and orange bitters? Or should we believe the plaque on the corner of Alhambra Street and Masonic Street in Martinez, Californa, claiming the first Martini was mixed there? Whatever the truth, there's no disputing the Martini's enduring popularity, and every bartender will tell you his is the real deal!

2 fl. oz. gin
Small wedge of lemon
2 drops of extra-dry white vermouth
1 green olive

Thoroughly chill the gin and a Martini glass, or place them in the freezer until very cold. Rub the edge of the glass with the lemon wedge. Pour in the gin and add the vermouth. Squeeze the juice from the lemon wedge into the glass. Serve immediately, decorated with a green olive on a cocktail stick while the drink is still really cold.

Serves 1

midori martini

see variations page 108

Sharply refreshing, a well-chilled Martini spiked with the tang of citrus is the perfect way to unwind after a long and exhausting day. Corporate whiz kid or not, you'll still feel like a million dollars as you raise the cool, frosted glass to your lips.

3 fl. oz. lemon vodka
1/2 fl. oz. Cointreau
1/2 fl. oz. Midori
Juice of 1/4 lemon
Ice cubes
Twist of lemon zest, to serve

Shake the vodka, Cointreau, Midori, and lemon juice together with plenty of ice cubes. Strain into a glass and serve decorated with a twist of lemon zest.

Serves 1

apple martini

see variations page 109

The classic Martini mix lends itself to all manner of exciting variations, and shaking vodka or gin with fruit liqueurs and juices works particularly well. Make sure both the bottles and the glass are very well chilled before starting to make the drink.

1 fl. oz. vodka or gin
1 fl. oz. Apple Schnapps
2 fl. oz. apple juice
1 tsp. lemon juice
Ice cubes
Green apple wedge, to serve

Put the vodka or gin, Apple Schnapps, apple juice, and lemon juice in a cocktail shaker. Add plenty of ice cubes and shake vigorously. Strain into a cocktail glass and serve decorated with a green apple wedge.

Serves 1

blue heaven martini

see variations page 110

Dreaming of tropical skies and deep blue seas? This classy cocktail will transport you to an exotic beach without the hassle of stepping on a plane. The drink can be stirred or shaken as you prefer.

3 fl. oz. vodka
1/2 fl. oz. Blue Curacao
Ice cubes
Maraschino cherry, to serve

Stir the vodka and Blue Curacao together with plenty of ice, or shake together with the ice in a cocktail shaker. Strain into a well-chilled cocktail glass and serve decorated with a maraschino cherry.

Serves 1

chocolate martini

see variations page 111

When an enterprising bartender created this creamy, frothy confection, he fulfilled every chocoholic's fantasy. Use dark bitter chocolate with at least 70% cocoa solids for a seriously indulgent hit.

2 small orange wedges
A little finely grated dark chocolate or
  equal quantities of cocoa powder and
  confectioners' sugar mixed together
2 fl. oz. vodka
1 oz. dark chocolate with at least
  70% cocoa solids
1 fl. oz. heavy cream
Ice cubes

Rub the rim of a well-chilled martini glass with one of the orange wedges. Dip it in the grated chocolate or cocoa powder and confectioners' sugar mixture. Chill the glass and the vodka bottle thoroughly. Put 1 oz. dark chocolate in a small bowl with the cream and microwave on low power until melted. Stir until smooth. Pour the vodka and melted chocolate mix into a cocktail shaker, add plenty of ice cubes, and shake well. Strain into the chocolate-rimmed glass and serve decorated with the second orange wedge.

Serves 1

variations

strawberry martini

see base recipe page 95

kiwi martini
Replace the strawberries with 1 teaspoon kiwifruit purée; the Crème de Fraise with kiwifruit liqueur; and the strawberry garnish with a slice of kiwifruit.

blueberry martini
Place 2 tablespoons fresh blueberries in a cocktail shaker. Crush the berries. Add 1 teaspoon sugar syrup, 2 fl. oz. vodka, and 3/4 fl. oz. Crème de Myrtille. Shake and strain into a glass. Decorate with blueberries on a cocktail stick.

prickly pear martini
Instead of the basic recipe, peel 1 prickly pear and push the flesh through a coarse metal sieve, or peel, remove the seeds, and blend to a purée. Put 1 teaspoon of the purée in a cocktail shaker with 3 fl. oz. tequila and the juice of 1/2 lime. Add plenty of ice and shake vigorously. Strain into a glass.

guava martini
Follow the directions for the Prickly Pear Martini, but use 1–2 guavas instead of a prickly pear.

mango martini
Follow the directions for the Prickly Pear Martini, but use 1 teaspoon puréed mango instead of a prickly pear.

variations

classic martini

see base recipe page 96

mr. bond
To re-create James Bond's favorite tipple, replace half the gin with vodka
and shake vigorously with the vermouth and plenty of ice cubes before
straining into the glass. Although shaking gin intensifies its juniper-like
flavor, it has no effect on the flavor of the vodka.

vodkatini
Replace the gin with vodka, pouring it into a Martini glass before dripping in
the vermouth. Stir and serve decorated with a small twist of lemon zest.

gibson
Serve the drink decorated with a pearl onion instead of an olive.

sake-tini
Use gin or vodka and shake with 1 tablespoon of sake and plenty of ice.
Strain into a Martini glass and decorate with a green olive and a thin strip
of cucumber peel threaded onto a cocktail stick.

sweet martini
Replace the dry vermouth with 1 fl. oz. sweet red vermouth. Shake with
plenty of ice. Strain into a Martini glass and decorate with a maraschino on
a stick.

variations

midori martini

see base recipe page 99

martini gold
Replace the vodka with tequila, the Midori with Grand Marnier, and the lemon juice with orange juice. Shake with the Cointreau and ice and strain into a glass.

st. clements martini
Replace the lemon vodka with orange vodka, Midori with orange bitters, and lemon juice with an orange wedge. Decorate with an orange zest twist.

grapefruit martini
Replace the lemon vodka with grapefruit vodka, the Cointreau and Midori with 1 fl. oz. dry white vermouth, and the lemon juice with 2 tablespoons grapefruit juice. Decorate with a grapefruit zest instead of lemon zest.

dry orange martini
Instead of the basic recipe, shake 3 fl. oz. bourbon, 1 fl. oz. Orange Curacao, 1 fl. oz. orange juice, and 1 tablespoon lemon juice with ice and strain into a glass. Decorate with a twist of orange zest instead of lemon zest.

mandarin martini
Instead of the basic recipe, shake 3 fl. oz. gin, 1 fl. oz. Triple Sec or Cointreau, and the juice of 1/2 a mandarin orange with plenty of ice and strain into a glass. Decorate with a thin slice of mandarin orange.

apple martini

see base recipe page 100

peach martini
Increase the vodka to 2 fl. oz. Replace the Apple Schnapps with Peach Schnapps and the apple juice with 1/2 fl. oz. of peach nectar. Decorate with a peach wedge instead of the apple wedge.

cherry martini
Shake 2 fl. oz. gin with 1/2 fl. oz. dry white vermouth, a couple of dashes of cherry brandy, 2 drops of Angostura, and plenty of ice.

apricot martini
Replace the Apple Schnapps with apricot brandy and the apple juice with orange juice. Decorate with a twist of orange and a slice of fresh apricot.

melon martini
Replace the Apple Schnapps with melon liquer, and replace the teaspoon of lemon juice with the juice of half a lime. Decorate with a small ball or a cube of melon on a stick.

cosmo martini
Replace the Apple Schnapps with Cointreau or Triple Sec; the apple juice with cranberry juice; and the teaspoon of lemon juice with the juice of half a lime. Decorate with a spiral of lime zest.

variations

blue heaven martini

see base recipe page 103

blue dawn martini
Pour the vodka into a well-chilled glass followed by the Blue Curacao. Let it stand until the Blue Curacao sinks to the bottom. Put the maraschino cherry on a cocktail stick to use as a stirrer before drinking.

blue sapphire martini
Replace the vodka with gin. Decorate with a twist of lemon zest instead of a cherry.

tequila blue martini
Replace the vodka with tequila. Decorate with a lime wedge instead of a cherry.

chili blue martini
Stir or shake 2 drops of Tabasco with the vodka and Blue Curacao. Float a small red chili in the glass, and omit the lime.

deep blue martini
Add a dash of Grenadine to the mix. Put the maraschino cherry and a blueberry on a cocktail stick.

chocolate martini

see base recipe page 104

white chocolate martini
Coat the rim of the glass with grated white chocolate, rather than dark or superfine sugar. Replace the 1 oz. dark chocolate with white chocolate.

chocolate orange martini
Replace the dark chocolate with orange-flavored dark chocolate, and add 1/2 fl. oz. Grand Marnier to the cocktail shaker.

mint chocolate martini
Follow the instructions for the White Chocolate Martini but add 1/2 fl. oz. Crème de Menthe liqueur to the cocktail shaker. Decorate with a short chocolate-covered peppermint stick.

chocca-mocca martini
Instead of preparing the basic recipe, shake 1 fl. oz. cold espresso coffee, 2 fl. oz. vodka, 1 fl. oz. Kahlúa, and 1 fl. oz. white or brown Crème de Cacao with plenty of ice. Strain into a glass that has been rimmed with chocolate.

chocolate banana martini
Instead of preparing the basic recipe, shake together 2 fl. oz. vodka with 1 fl. oz. Crème de Banane and 1 fl. oz. white Crème de Cacao with plenty of ice. Strain into a cocktail glass. Decorate the side of the glass with a slice of banana.

sparkle & fizz

Nothing puts you in the party mood quite like a glass of bubbly, and this mix of sparklers make the ultimate good-time drinks. If you can't afford the best Dom Perignon, don't fret; they all taste just as good topped off with your favorite sparkling wine.

mimosa

see variations page 127

Champagne hasn't earned its nickname "giggle wine" for nothing, as no other drink can match it for making a party go with a swing. If the genuine article is beyond your budget, substitute a good sparkling wine such as Cava.

1 fl. oz. freshly squeezed orange juice
2 tsp. Orange Curacao or Grand Marnier
1/2 cup (4 fl. oz.) champagne

Pour the orange juice into a well-chilled champagne flute to fill it by about one-quarter. Add the Orange Curacao or Grand Marnier and top off with champagne. Stir and serve immediately.

Serves 1

champagne cocktail

see variations page 128

This is one of the easiest cocktails to mix, because it requires no special skills or equipment — beyond a steady hand! A drink similar to today's champagne cocktail first appeared in 1862 in Jerry Thomas's *How to Mix Drinks* cocktail book; but it didn't catch on until 1899, when John Dougherty submitted a version of the cocktail to a New York competition. To re-create John Dougherty's original drink, rub the sugar cube over the zest of an orange before adding it to the glass. When pouring the champagne, reduce its froth by holding the glass at a 45-degree angle.

1 sugar cube
2 dashes of Angostura bitters
3/4 fl. oz. brandy
6 fl. oz. champagne
Slice of orange and maraschino cherry, to serve

Put the sugar cube in a well-chilled champagne flute, add the Angostura, and let it soak for a few minutes. Pour in the brandy and top off with the champagne. Decorate the glass with a slice of orange and a maraschino cherry.

Serves 1

wild hibiscus royale

see variations page 129

Australian wild hibiscus flowers preserved in syrup make an unusual and eye-catching addition to a celebration drink. If the petals stubbornly remain closed, push a maraschino cherry into the center of the flower to encourage them to open and to hold them in place. Jars of the flowers can be bought from gourmet shops or the Internet.

1 wild hibiscus flower
1/2 tsp. rose water
1/4 pt. champagne
1 tbsp. hibiscus syrup from the jar

Carefully place the hibiscus flower at the bottom of a well-chilled champagne flute, making sure it stands upright. Add the rose water, top off with the champagne, and finally drizzle in the syrup.

Serves 1

framboise kir royale

see variations page 130

Perfect for an alfresco summer party when soft fruits are at their sweetest and most fragrant. Because raspberries freeze well, this warm-weather sparkler can be enjoyed all year.

1 fl. oz. Crème de Framboise
4 1/2 fl. oz. well-chilled champagne
Fresh raspberries, to serve

Pour the Crème de Framboise into a frosted champagne flute and top off with well-chilled champagne. Float a few raspberries in the drink and serve at once.

Serves 1

gin rickey

see variations page 131

Believed to have been created in the late nineteenth century for political lobbyist Joe Rickey, who was a regular at Shoemaker's Restaurant in Washington DC. The original Rickey mix contained no sugar — just lime juice, gin, and a squirt of soda — but a little Grenadine takes the sharp edge off the drink, and gives it a pretty pink hue.

2 fl. oz. gin
1 tsp. Grenadine syrup
Juice of 1/2 lime or 1/2 small lemon
Soda water
Lime and/or lemon slices, to serve

Half-fill a tall glass with ice. Mix the gin and Grenadine together and pour over the ice. Add the lime or lemon juice and top off with soda water. Decorate the glass with lime and/or lemon slices.

Serves 1

royale blue

see variations page 132

Another cool sparkler that makes the most of Blue Curacao's dazzling hue. A kiwifruit makes a spectacular decoration, but if it's unavailable, tuck a string of red currants, black currants, or white currants over the side of the glass instead.

1 fl. oz. Blue Curacao
1/2 cup (4 fl. oz.) champagne, well chilled
Slice of kiwifruit

Pour the Blue Curacao into a frosted champagne flute and top off with the well-chilled champagne. Decorate the side of the glass with a slice of kiwifruit.

Serves 1

black velvet

see variations page 133

Champagne was a popular celebration drink in upper-class Victorian England, but in 1861 the sudden death of the Queen's Consort, Prince Albert, plunged the whole country into mourning. Still wanting to serve champagne but feeling it should be in mourning too, the bartender at Brooks's Club in London combined it with Guinness as a suitably somber way to mark the occasion. He dubbed the cocktail Black Velvet and served it in a beer tankard, but today a goblet or champagne flute is normally used. The drink became a favorite of Prince Otto von Bismarck, and in Germany it is known by his name.

3 fl. oz. Guinness, well chilled
3 fl. oz. champagne, well chilled

Both the Guinness and champagne must be chilled thoroughly. Pour the Guinness into a goblet or champagne flute and then carefully add the champagne, pouring it over the back of a spoon so it floats on top of the Guinness. Serve with a stirrer or drink with the layers still separate.

Serves 1

bellini

see variations page 134

An exhibition during the 1940s of paintings by the Venetian artist Bellini prompted Giuseppi Cipriani, the bartender of the legendary Harry's Bar in Venice, to mark the occasion with this champagne and peach juice cocktail. A true Bellini is made with fresh white peaches, but because their season is short, most amateur bartenders resort to using the more readily available yellow-fleshed fruit — unless, of course, they've stocked their freezer with enough white peach juice to see them through the year. Prosecco, the Italian sparkling wine, is used in this recipe instead of the original champagne.

1 fresh white peach
Juice of 1/4 lemon
1 tbsp. orange juice
1/2 cup (4 fl. oz.) Prosecco

Put the peach in a bowl and cover it with boiling water. Leave for 1–2 minutes, then drain and cool under cold water. Nick the skin in several places with the point of a sharp knife, and remove the skin with your fingers. Cut the peach in half and remove the pit. Chop the flesh; place it in a blender with the lemon juice and orange juice; and blend until smooth. Fill a well-chilled champagne flute one-quarter full with the peach juice (freeze the rest for another occasion) and top off with Prosecco.

Serves 1

passion fruit bellini

see variations page 135

Not only does this cocktail look beautiful, but its intoxicating flavor and aroma will instantly transport you to a world of white coral beaches and warm blue seas. Prosecco can be used instead of champagne, if you wish.

2 passion fruit
2 fl. oz. freshly squeezed orange juice
5 fl. oz. champagne

Halve the passion fruit and scoop out the seeds and pulp into a small bowl or pan. Add the orange juice and heat gently in the microwave or on a low burner until the passion fruit seeds separate from the pulp. Strain and cool. Put enough of the passion fruit mix into a well-chilled champagne flute to fill by one-quarter and top off with champagne.

Serves 1

mimosa

see base recipe page 113

mimosa blush
Use blush- or blood-orange juice in place of ordinary orange juice.

mango mimosa
Replace the orange juice with mango nectar and drop a fresh raspberry in the drink.

lychee mimosa
Replace the Orange Curacao with Lychee Liqueur.

lemon mimosa
Replace the Orange Curacao with Limoncello.

variations

champagne cocktail

see base recipe page 114

red devil champagne cocktail
Omit the sugar cube and bitters. Replace the brandy with cherry brandy
and add the same quantity of cranberry juice, before topping off with
champagne.

amaretto champagne cocktail
Omit the sugar cube and bitters. Replace the brandy with 2 teaspoons
Amaretto Disaronno and 2 teaspoons Cointreau and a squeeze of lime juice,
before topping off with champagne

just peachy champagne cocktail
Replace the brandy with bourbon. Add 1/2 fl. oz. peach liqueur to the mix
before topping off with champagne.

apricot champagne cocktail
Replace the brandy with apricot brandy.

variations

wild hibiscus royale

see base recipe page 117

rose petal royale
Omit the hibiscus flower and syrup. Pour the rose water (or replace it with a dash of Grenadine) in a well-chilled flute and top off with champagne. Float a couple of washed pink rose petals on top.

borage blossom royale
Omit the hibiscus flower, syrup, and rose water. Add a dash of Crème de Cassis to a well-chilled flute and top off with champagne. Float 2 or 3 blue borage flowers on top.

violette royale
Omit the hibiscus flower, syrup, and rose water. Pour champagne into a well-chilled flute and dribble in Crème de Violette liqueur. Decorate with a violet floated on top.

lavender royale
Omit the hibiscus flower, syrup, and rose water. Add a dash of lavender liqueur or cordial to a well-chilled flute and top off with champagne. Decorate with a short sprig of lavender flowers balanced across the top of the glass.

sparkle & fizz   129

variations

framboise kir royale

see base recipe page 118

dry orange royale
Replace the Crème de Framboise with Orange Curacao. Float a thin strip of orange zest tied in a knot in the glass.

wild strawberry liqueur
Replace the Crème de Framboise with Crème de Fraise des Bois (wild strawberry liqueur) or Crème de Fraise. Float a few wild strawberries or a thin strawberry slice in the drink.

cassis royale
Replace the Crème de Framboise with Crème de Cassis, and hook a small bunch of black currants over the side of the glass.

cherry ripe royale
Replace the Crème de Framboise with cherry brandy or Crème de Cerise. Hook 2 cherries joined at the stalk over the side of the glass.

variations

gin rickey

see base recipe page 120

rickey fizz
Shake the gin with the lemon juice and 1 teaspoon sugar syrup. Omit the Grenadine. Pour over ice in a tall glass, top off with soda water, and add a little extra lemon juice for a sharper, citrusy taste. Serve with a straw.

silver rickey fizz
Follow the directions for the Rickey Fizz, but add a little lightly whisked egg white to the shaker to give the finished drink a frothier head.

vodka rickey
Substitute vodka for the gin and the juice from one-quarter orange in for the lime or lemon juice. Decorate the glass with an orange slice instead of the lime of lemon slices.

tequila rickey
Substitute tequila for the gin. Use lime juice and a lime wedge instead of lemon juice and a lemon slice.

royale blue

see base recipe page 121

sparkling apple blue
Replace the champagne with sparkling apple juice or cider.

blue spritz
Replace the champagne with 2 fl. oz. dry white wine and 2. fl. oz. soda water.

purple patch
For a dense purple sparkler, replace the champagne with Sparkling Shiraz red wine.

elderflower blue
Instead of champagne, use 1 tablespoon elderflower cordial and top off the glass with sparkling white wine or soda water.

variations

black velvet

see base recipe page 122

somerset velvet
Substitute cider for the champagne, but add it first, with the Guinness as the top layer.

lemon velvet
Substitute lemonade for the champagne.

top hat
Substitute ginger beer for the champagne (or ginger ale).

royal purple velvet
Pour 2 teaspoons black currant cordial into a champagne flute before adding the Guinness followed by the champagne.

variations

bellini

see base recipe page 125

apricot bellini
Replace the peach with 2 ripe apricots.

strawberry bellini
Replace the peach with 4 large, ripe strawberries.

blackbery bellini
Instead of preparing the basic recipe, put 3 or 4 frozen blackberries in a champagne flute and add 2 teaspoons Créme de Mure. Top off with Prosecco.

raspberry bellini
Instead of preparing the basic recipe, put 3 or 4 frozen raspberries in a champagne flute and add 2 teaspoons Crème de Framboise. Top off with Prosecco.

variations

passion fruit bellini

see base recipe page 126

kiwi bellini
Blend 1 peeled kiwifruit with the orange juice and pour enough into a well-chilled champagne flute to fill by one quarter. Top off with champagne.

lychee bellini
Blend 4 peeled and pitted fresh lychees (or 4 canned lychees, drained) with the orange juice and pour enough into a well-chilled champagne flute to fill by one quarter. Top off with champagne.

mango bellini
Blend 1/2 ripe mango with 2 fl. oz. mango nectar and pour enough into a well-chilled champagne flute to fill by one quarter. Top off with champagne.

papaya bellini
Blend 1/2 ripe, deseeded papaya with the orange juice and pour enough into a well-chilled champagne flute to fill by one quarter. Top off with champagne.

shots, shooters & sours

When Frank Sinatra crooned "set 'em up Joe," if the

bartender had mixed him one of these cocktails,

Ol' Blue Eyes would instantly have cheered up.

Cocktails don't come more stylish than a Black

Russian; Caipirinha and Pisco Sour evoke Carnival's

exhilaration; and the B-52 is always a bombshell.

pisco sour

see variations page 152

The national drink of Peru and Chile, Pisco is a brandy distilled from locally grown grapes. It is traditionally shaken with sugar syrup, lime juice, egg white, and Angostura to make a Pisco Sour. In Chilean bars, regulars often drink Pisco neat poured over ice, something the average tourist would be wise to avoid!

2 fl. oz. Pisco
1 tbsp. sugar syrup
2 fl. oz. freshly squeezed lime juice
About 1 tsp. egg white
Dash of Angostura bitters
Ice cubes
Pinch of freshly grated nutmeg

Put the Pisco, sugar syrup, lime juice, egg white, Angostura, and half a dozen ice cubes in a cocktail shaker; shake vigorously. Strain into a cocktail glass, and serve with a pinch of freshly grated nutmeg sprinkled on top.

Serves 1

caipirinha

see variations page 153

Peru and Chile might have Pisco, but Brazil can claim an equally potent liquor as its national drink — Cachaca (pronounced kah-sha-sah), a rum-like white spirit distilled from pressed sugarcane. On hot sunny days the beautiful and tanned people packing Copacabana beach keep cool sipping this refreshing citrus cocktail. The lime is always muddled with the sugar, never squeezed straight into the glass.

1 lime
2 tsp. superfine or demerera sugar
Ice cubes
2 fl. oz. Cachaca

Cut the lime into small pieces and place in a tumbler. Add the sugar and, with a muddler, crush the lime to release its aroma and juice and dissolve the sugar. Fill the glass with ice cubes and pour in the Cachaca. Serve with a stirrer.

Serves 1

rum sour

see variations page 154

The lush Caribbean island of Jamaica is famous for its rum, and most visitors are more than happy to drink this liquid gold. Spiked with freshly squeezed lemon juice and poured over plenty of ice, this tangy drink makes an easy and very refreshing sundowner.

1 1/2 fl. oz. light Jamaican rum
3/4 fl. oz. freshly squeezed lime juice
1 tsp. superfine sugar or sugar syrup
Ice cubes
Slice of lime and maraschino cherries,
to decorate

Put the rum, lime juice, sugar or syrup, and ice cubes in a cocktail shaker. Shake vigorously. Strain into a short glass and decorate with a lime slice and maraschino cherries.

Serves 1

black russian

see variations page 155

At the height of the Cold War in 1949, Gustave Tops, the bartender at the Hotel Metropole in Brussels, created this blend of vodka and coffee liqueur for one of his favorite clients, Perle Mesta. The lively socialite was America's lady ambassador to Luxembourg at the time.

Ice cubes
2 fl. oz. vodka
1 fl. oz. Kahlúa or Tia Maria

Put 4 or 5 ice cubes in a short glass or low tumbler or use a couple of tablespoons of crushed ice. Add the vodka, followed by the Kahlúa or Tia Maria, and stir well. Serve with a stirrer.

Serves 1

whiskey sour

see variations page 156

Sours — cocktails sharpened with a good shot of citrus juice — date from 1850s America, when they were made with brandy. Today, whiskey, usually bourbon or Irish whiskey rather than Scotch, is more popular, but any spirit can be used. It's important to use freshly squeezed lemon juice to achieve the necessary "sour" flavor.

2 fl. oz. bourbon
Juice of 1/2 lemon
1 tsp. sugar syrup
Ice cubes
Lemon and lime zest, to serve

Put the bourbon, lemon juice, and sugar syrup in a cocktail shaker; add half a dozen ice cubes; and shake vigorously. Strain into a cocktail glass, and serve decorated with strips of lemon and lime zest.

Serves 1

lime shooter

see variations page 157

If you prefer a long drink that you can sip and savor, shooters are definitely not for you!
As their name suggests, these cocktails are served in small, straight glasses that have a
capacity of little more than a mouthful. If you're with a group of friends, line up the
shooters on the bar, toast each other in unison, and toss the contents of the glass down
in one.

1 fl. oz. white rum
Juice of 1 lime
1 tbsp. orange juice
1 tbsp. light cream
Ice cubes
Lime wedge, to serve

Put the rum, lime juice, orange juice, and cream in a cocktail shaker; add half a dozen ice
cubes; and shake vigorously. Strain into a shot glass and decorate with a lime wedge on top.
Before tossing down the drink, remove the lime wedge and squeeze it into the glass.

Serves 1

b-52

see variations page 158

Layered drinks are guaranteed to elicit gasps of admiration and a round of applause from your guests, and the B-52, named after the long-range bomber aircraft used in the Vietnam War, is one of the most popular. Various establishments lay claim to its invention; these include the famous Alice's Restaurant on Malibu pier in California, unintentionally immortalized by Arlo Guthrie in his '60s hit single about his friend Alice.

1/2 fl. oz. Kahlúa
1/2 fl. oz. Bailey's Irish Cream liqueur
1/2 fl. oz. Grand Marnier

Pour the Kahlúa into a small well-chilled glass such as a sherry or shot glass. Gently drizzle the Bailey's on top of the Kahlúa over the back of a spoon, followed by the Grand Marnier, again pouring it gently over the spoon. Leave for a short while to give the layers time to settle. Serve with a stirrer or sip the drink so you can enjoy each layer.

Serves 1

americano

see variations page 159

The Americano was created in the 1860s by Gaspare Campari at his Campari Bar. Later it became the inspiration for another classic cocktail, the Negroni, where gin was added to the original mix. Gaspare christened his creation a Milano-Torino — Milan being home to Campari and Turin where Cinzano produced its sweet red vermouth. During the years of Prohibition, the number of Americans visiting the bar soared and the cocktail was subsequently renamed the Americano in their honor.

1 fl. oz. Campari
1 fl. oz. sweet red vermouth
Ice cubes
Splash of soda water
Twists of orange and lemon, to serve

Pour the Campari followed by the vermouth into a tumbler glass half-filled with ice cubes. Add a dash of soda water. Decorate with twists of orange and lemon.

Serves 1

variations

pisco sour

see base recipe page 137

pisco not-so-sour
Substitute freshly squeezed orange or mandarin orange juice for the
lime juice.

in the pink pisco
Substitute Grenadine for the sugar syrup.

pisco fizz
Strain the drink into a highball glass and top off with soda water.

piscola
Pour the amount of Pisco into a tumbler half-filled with ice, and top off with
cola. Add a twist of lemon and serve with a straw.

ginger pisco
Pour the amount of Pisco into a tumbler half-filled with ice, and top off with
ginger ale. Add a twist of lime and serve with a straw.

variations

caipirinha

see base recipe page 138

orange caipirinha
Substitute one quarter of a thin-skinned orange or half a mandarin orange for the lime.

mango caipirinha
Substitute the chopped flesh of half a ripe, fragrant mango for the lime.

pineapple caipirinha
Substitute a small wedge of pineapple (peeled, chopped, and any hard core cut away) for the lime.

caipirodka
The drink can be also made with vodka instead of Cachaca. Instead of lime, muddle half a fresh peach with the sugar.

caipirquila
Replace the Cachaca with tequila and the lime with 2 passion fruit. Muddle the pulp of the passion fruit with half the quantity of sugar. The seeds can be left in or removed from the pulp as preferred. To separate the pulp from the seeds, warm it first so the seeds come away easily.

rum sour

see base recipe page 141

lemon rum sour
Prepare the basic recipe, but replace the lime juice with the freshly squeezed juice of half a lemon. Instead of decorating with lemon and lime zest, serve with a wedge of orange and squeeze it into the glass before drinking.

amaretto rum sour
Prepare the basic recipe, but use 3/4 fl. oz. of rum and the same amount amaretto liqueur. Add a few drops of Angostura bitters to the mix.

rum sour float
Prepare the basic recipe, but stir the lime juice and sugar together until the sugar dissolves. Pour into a tumbler three-quarters filled with ice cubes and float the rum on top. Stir before drinking.

rum apple sour
Prepare the basic recipe, but use equal quantities of rum and Sour Apple liqueur and add 2 teaspoons Triple Sec or Orange Curacao. Drop slices of apple and orange into the glass and omit the lemon and lime zest.

rum apricot sour
Prepare the basic recipe, but replace half the rum with apricot brandy.

variations

black russian

see base recipe page 142

white russian
Float 1 fl. oz. lightly whipped heavy cream or thick coconut milk on top of the finished drink.

tall black russian
Pour the vodka and Kahlúa or Tia Maria over ice in a highball glass, and top off with cola.

black russian of irish extraction
Pour the vodka and Kahlúa or Tia Maria over ice in a highball glass, and add a head of Guinness.

voodoo brew
Substitute white rum for the vodka.

mexican brew
Substitute tequila for the vodka.

variations

whiskey sour

see base recipe page 145

sour whiskey frizz
Add half a lightly beaten egg white to the shaker to give the finished drink a frothy head.

brandy sour
Substitute brandy for the bourbon and a maraschino cherry and an orange slice for the lemon and lime zest.

whiskey cola sour
Strain the drink into a highball glass and top off with cola.

whiskey ginger sour
Strain the drink into a highball glass and top off with ginger ale.

berry sour
Replace the bourbon with plain vodka and shake with the other ingredients, adding a dash of Crème de Cassis. Strain into a highball glass and top off with cranberry juice.

variations

lime shooter

see base recipe page 146

vodka lime shooter
Substitute plain vodka for the white rum.

minty lime shooter
Replace the orange juice with the same quantity of green Crème de Menthe.

golden shooter
Use tequila instead of white rum and replace the orange juice with mango nectar.

bourbon shooter
Replace the white rum with bourbon.

lime slammer
Pour the rum (or replace it with tequila) into a shooter glass, and add the same amount of lemonade and a small squeeze of lime juice. Put your hand over the top of the glass, hold the glass firmly, and slam it down on a hard surface. The mix will bubble, turn white, and should be tossed down in one gulp.

variations

b-52

see base recipe page 149

flaming b-52
Although flaming a cocktail is great bar showmanship — it should be approached with caution. Substitute dark, overproof rum (60–80%) for Grand Marnier and use a heatproof glass. Fill to the top, ignite the drink, and blow out just before drinking.

b-53
Replace the Grand Marnier with plain vodka. Pour the vodka into the glass first, followed by the Kahlúa and finally by the Bailey's Irish Cream.

b-54
Replace the Grand Marnier with Amaretto Disaronno. Pour into the glass first, followed by the Kahlúa and finally by the Bailey's Irish Cream.

b-special
Replace the Bailey's with Amarula Cream liqueur. Pour it into the glass after the Kahlúa and before the Grand Marnier.

b-banana
In the following order layer equal quantities of, Amaretto Disaronno, Crème de Banane, and Amarula Cream or Bailey's Irish Cream.

variations

americano

see base recipe page 151

americano refresher
Pour the Campari and vermouth into a highball glass half-filled with ice and top off with soda water to make a long drink.

americano bianco
Substitute sweet white vermouth for the red.

dry americano
Substitute Noilly Prat Dry White Vermouth for the red.

orange americano
Top off with orange juice rather than soda — add a dash for a short drink or more for a long, refreshing cocktail.

lemon americano
Substitute Noilly Prat Dry White Vermouth for the red and add a dash of lemonade.

summer sizzlers

Summer is the perfect time to enjoy a cool,

refreshing cocktail, and this chapter has something

for everyone — whether you crave an ice-cold

Daiquiri, a chilled fruit-packed Pimm's, a tangy Mint

Julep, or a crystal flute of sparkling Buck's Fizz.

white wine strawberry spritzer

see variations page 178

Marinating the strawberries in the wine for one hour gives the wine time to absorb their sweet, scented flavor. If you want a less alcoholic drink, increase the quantity of mineral or soda water.

1 large or 2 small strawberries, hulled and
    chopped
3 fl. oz. dry white wine, such as Pinot Grigio
Dash of Crème de Fraise
3 fl. oz. sparkling mineral or soda water, well
    chilled
1 kiwifruit slice, to serve

Put the strawberries in a large wine glass or highball glass and add the white wine. Leave in the fridge for one hour, muddling occasionally. Add the Crème de Fraise, stir well, and top off with the sparkling mineral water or soda water. Decorate the glass with the kiwifruit slice and serve at once.

Serves 1

viva sangria

see variations page 179

Relaxing days by the pool followed by romantic nights under the stars — there's no better way to relive the pleasures of that lazy, hazy Spanish break than with a glass of this refreshing summer drink. If mixing jugs of Sangria for a party, avoid making them more than 2 hours before serving. Keep the jugs tightly covered with plastic wrap, or the red wine will start to oxidize and the drink will lose its freshness.

Ice cubes
Fresh fruit slices, such as lemon, orange, apple,
    pineapple, and fig
1 tbsp. brandy
3 fl. oz. well-chilled red wine
3 fl. oz. lemonade

Half-fill a tall glass with ice cubes and drop in the slices of fresh fruit. Add the brandy and red wine and then slowly pour in the lemonade. Stir well before drinking.

Serves 1

bronx

see variations page 180

Johnny Solon, the bartender of New York's Waldorf Astoria hotel during the early 1900s, took credit for inventing the Bronx cocktail in 1906 when the hotel was just known simply as the Waldorf, and it stood on the site where the Empire State Building is today. Asked by a customer one night to create a new cocktail for him, Johnny christened his gin, vermouth, and orange juice concoction a "Bronx." Quizzed over the name, he replied his inspiration had come from a recent visit to the Bronx Zoo where he'd seen so many strange creatures it was impossible to tell the difference between the zoo and his bar.

2 fl. oz. gin
2 tsp. sweet red vermouth
2 tsp. dry white vermouth
2 tbsp. freshly squeezed orange juice
Ice cubes
Orange wedges and a maraschino cherry, to
    serve

Put the gin, red vermouth, white vermouth, and orange juice in a cocktail shaker with ice cubes. Shake well. Three-quarters fill a glass, and strain in the drink. Serve with a stirrer and a straw and decorate the glass with orange wedges and a maraschino cherry.

Serves 1

strawberry pimm's

see variations page 181

Fruit salad in a glass tankard is how many fans think of Pimm's No. 1 Cup. This gin-based cocktail mix grew from humble beginnings as a house specialty during the 1840s at James Pimm's London Oyster Bar. It has grown to become a permanent fixture on today's English social calendar, enjoyed at all the best Henley, Ascot, and Wimbledon parties. Fresh strawberries muddled with the traditional mix add a refreshing, summery flavor. Mixed in a pitcher, this makes a good alfresco party drink — increase the quantities according to the number of your guests.

3–4 strawberries, roughly chopped
2 fl. oz. Pimm's No. 1 Cup
About 3/4 cup (6 fl. oz.) lemonade
Ice cubes
Lemon, orange, and apple slices
Extra small, whole strawberries
Cucumber batons or strips of peel
Fresh mint sprigs

Put the chopped strawberries in a glass tankard or tall glass and pour over the Pimm's. Crush the strawberries with a muddler, or the back of a spoon. Add 4 or 5 ice cubes and top off with lemonade. Stir them, drop in lemon, orange, and apple slices, small whole strawberries, cucumber batons or strips of peel, and fresh mint sprigs.

Serves 1

berry breeze

see variations page 182

A relaxing way to watch the late summer sun go down when you're chilling out after a busy day.

3 strawberries
6 blackberries
2 fl. oz. gin
1/2 fl. oz. Crème de Cassis
1/2 fl. oz. strawberry syrup
Ice cubes
1/2 cup (4 fl. oz.) lemonade
Extra strawberries and blackberries, to serve

Muddle the strawberries and blackberries in a large measuring cup with the gin, Crème de Cassis, and strawberry syrup. Strain into a tall glass three-quarters filled with ice cubes and top off with the lemonade. Serve decorated with extra strawberries and blackberries.

Serves 1

papaya frappé

see variations page 183

Get a refreshing flavor of the tropics with this long, cooling drink. When buying exotic fruit, check its ripeness by smelling it. If the fruit smells sweet and fragrant, that's how it will taste; but if it has no scent, it will probably have no taste either.

1/4 ripe papaya, peeled, deseeded, and chopped
1 tbsp. crushed ice
2 tbsp. freshly squeezed orange juice
Juice of 1/2 a lime
4 1/2 fl. oz. sparkling wine
Fresh flowers, to decorate

Put the papaya, crushed ice, orange juice, and freshly squeezed lime juice in a blender, and blend until smooth. Strain into a champagne flute and carefully pour in the sparkling wine. Stir and serve immediately, decorated with a fresh exotic flower such as an orchid bloom.

Serves 1

mint julep

see variations page 184

The first record of a mint julep being enjoyed — seemingly for its medicinal qualities — dates from 1803, when John Davis, an Englishman working as a tutor in Virginia at one of the great Southern plantation houses, wrote of "a dram of spirituous liquor that has mint in it, taken by Virginians of a morning." Today the mint julep is synonymous with the Kentucky Derby. More than 80,000 are downed at the annual two-day event.

4 fresh mint leaves
1 tsp. superfine sugar
1 tsp. cold water
Crushed ice
2 fl. oz. bourbon
Mint sprigs, to serve

Put the mint leaves in the bottom of a highball glass. Add the sugar and water and muddle together to crush the leaves and release their flavor. Spoon crushed ice into the glass until it is three-quarters full. Add the bourbon and serve the drink with a straw and stirrer, decorated with fresh mint sprigs.

Serves 1

pomegranate margarita

see variations page 185

It's not surprising that many bartenders have claimed they created the Margarita, one of the world's most famous cocktails. Carlos "Danny" Herrera's case is certainly one of the most colorful. In the late 1930s American showgirl Marjorie King was a regular customer at Herrera's Bar, Mexico. Marjorie was allergic to all spirits apart from tequila, and, because she refused to drink it straight, Danny struggled to serve her. One night he came up with the idea of blending tequila and Cointreau with fresh lime juice and crushed ice, a concoction he dubbed "Margarita," the Mexican version of Marjorie.

4 fl. oz. pomegranate juice
Splash of Grenadine for added color (optional)
1 fl. oz. freshly squeezed lime juice, plus extra
    for dipping
Fine or coarse sea salt
1/2 fl. oz. Triple Sec
1 fl. oz. tequila
Pomegranate seeds

Pour the pomegranate juice (and Grenadine, if using) into a shallow container and freeze until ice crystals form. Dip the rim of a cocktail glass in lime juice and then into salt until it is evenly coated. Break up the frozen pomegranate juice until it is slushy. Place in a cocktail shaker with 1 fl. oz. lime juice, the Triple Sec, and tequila. Shake vigorously and strain into the glass. Float a few pomegranate seeds in the drink and serve.

Serves 1

in the pink buck's fizz

see variations page 186

The original Buck's Fizz, made by mixing two-thirds champagne with one-third freshly squeezed orange juice, was created after World War I by a Mr. McGarry, the bartender at the time of Buck's Club in London's Mayfair. Very specific about the proportions of his drink, he would no doubt have frowned on any upstart adding a dash of Grenadine, but the resulting pink glow makes this cocktail the ultimate romantic tipple, perfect for Valentine's Day or a special evening in.

About 1/2 cup (4 fl. oz.) champagne
About 2 fl. oz. freshly squeezed orange juice,
    well chilled
Dash of Grenadine

Chill the champagne and orange juice thoroughly. Pour the orange juice into a frosted champagne flute to fill by one-third and slowly top off with champagne. Add a dash of Grenadine and serve at once.

Serves 1

frozen banana daiquiri

see variations page 187

Sixteen years after the first daiquiris were downed in Cuba, the La Floridita Bar in Havana added crushed ice to create the world's first frozen daiquiri. Depending on the ripeness and sweetness of the fruit used, you may need to add a little sugar syrup to the finished cocktail.

1 1/2 fl. oz. white rum
3/4 fl. oz. Crème de Banane liqueur
4 tsp. freshly squeezed lime juice
1/2 medium banana, peeled and roughly
    chopped
Crushed ice
Lime wedges and extra banana slices, to
    decorate

Measure the rum, Crème de Banane, and lime juice into a blender, add the chopped bananas, and blend for about 10 seconds. Add 2–3 tablespoons of crushed ice and blend for 30 seconds more. Pour into a large wine glass. Pop a couple of short straws into the glass and serve decorated with a wedge of lime and a slice of banana tucked over the side.

Serves 1

white wine strawberry spritzer

see base recipe page 161

melon spritz
Substitute a little chopped honeydew melon for the strawberries, and substitute melon liqueur for the Crème de Fraise.

just peachy spritz
Substitute a quarter of a peeled yellow peach for the strawberries, and substitute Peach Schnapps for the Crème de Fraise.

strawberry elderflower spritz
Replace the Crème de Fraise with elderflower cordial and use lime- or lemon-flavored sparkling water rather than plain. Decorate the glass with a twist of citrus peel instead of kiwifruit.

raspberry spritz
Marinate 4 gently crushed raspberries instead of strawberries in the wine, and replace the Crème de Fraise with Crème de Framboise or Crème de Cassis.

viva sangria

see base recipe page 162

sangria spritz
Replace the lemonade with 1 fl. oz. orange juice and 2 fl. oz. soda water or sparkling mineral water. Sweeten to taste with a dash of sugar syrup.

sweet apple sangria
Replace the lemonade with sparkling apple juice.

sangria sunrise
Rather than brandy, use an orange liqueur such as Cointreau or Grand Marnier.

sangria with a tropical twist
Use white rum instead of brandy, and use slices of lime and fresh mango instead of lemon, orange, apple, and fig.

bronx

see base recipe page 165

dry bronx
Omit the sweet vermouth and increase the amount of dry vermouth to 3/4 fl. oz. or 4 teaspoons.

long cool bronx
Halve the amounts of gin, sweet vermouth, and dry vermouth. Shake with the orange juice, and strain into a long glass over ice, and top off with soda or tonic water.

vodka bronx
Replace the gin with vodka.

johnny solon's bronx
The original Bronx mix omitted the dry vermouth. It was made by shaking 2 1/2 fl. oz. gin with 1/2 fl. oz. sweet red vermouth and 1/2 fl. oz. freshly squeezed orange juice.

strawberry pimm's

see base recipe page 166

apple pimm's
Replace the lemonade with sparkling apple juice.

raspberry and red currant pimm's
Muddle 4 raspberries and 2 sprigs of red currants (strip the currants from the stalks) with the Pimm's before topping off with lemonade. Serve decorated with a small sprig of red currants draped over the side of the glass.

pimms with a punch
Pep up the mix by adding 1/2 fl. oz. gin or vodka along with the Pimm's and lemonade.

winter pimm's
Because Pimm's No. 1 Cup is a summer drink, in winter try lightly spiced Pimm's No. 3 Cup. Warm 2 fl. oz. Pimm's No. 3 Cup with 6 fl. oz. apple juice, 2 whole cloves, and half a cinnamon stick until almost boiling. Pour into a heatproof tankard or tall glass, add orange and apple slices, and serve.

berry breeze

see base recipe page 168

ginger breeze
Top off with ginger ale rather than lemonade.

orchard breeze
Top off with sparkling apple juice rather than lemonade.

elderflower breeze
Instead of adding lemonade, add 1 tablespoon elderflower cordial and top off with sparkling mineral water or soda water.

cherry breeze
Replace the strawberries with 6 pitted cherries and the blackberries with raspberries. Muddle with the gin, substituting Crème de Framboise for the Crème de Cassis and Kirsch for the strawberry syrup. Strain over ice into a tall glass and top off with either lemonade or soda water. Serve decorated with fresh cherries and raspberries instead of stawberrries and blackberries.

papaya frappé

see base recipe page 169

mango frappé
Substitute half a ripe mango, peeled and chopped, for the papaya.

lychee frappé
Substitute 4 peeled and pitted fresh lychees (or 4 canned lychees, drained) for the papaya.

watermelon frappé
Substitute a small wedge of peeled watermelon, deseeded and chopped, for the papaya.

coconut frappé
Replace the papaya with 3 fl. oz. thick coconut milk and the orange juice with pineapple juice.

mint julep

see base recipe page 170

brandy mint julep
Substitute brandy for the bourbon.

crème de menthe julep
Instead of the basic recipe, stir the bourbon with 1/2 fl. oz. green or white Crème de Menthe, then pour into a glass over crushed ice. Decorate with fresh mint sprigs.

sour julep
Muddle the mint leaves with the sugar and 1 fl. oz. of lime juice (instead of water). Add crushed ice and pour over the bourbon. Decorate with fresh mint sprigs.

tequila julep
Substitute tequila for the bourbon.

pomegranate margarita

see base recipe page 173

classic margarita
Coat the rim of the glass as in the basic recipe. Put 2 fl. oz. tequila in a
cocktail shaker with 1 fl. oz. Triple Sec, 1 fl. oz. lime juice, and plenty of
ice cubes. Shake vigorously. Strain into the glass. Alternatively, put the
ingredients in a blender, add crushed ice, and blend before pouring straight
into the glass.

blue margarita
Follow the instructions for the Classic Margarita, but substitute Blue Curacao
for the Triple Sec.

kiwi margarita
Frost the rim of the glass with sugar, if preferred. Put 1 fl. oz. tequila, 2 fl. oz.
pineapple juice, 1 fl. oz. Triple Sec, 1 fl. oz. lime juice, and 1 peeled, chopped
kiwifruit into a blender. Add crushed ice and blend. Pour into a cocktail glass.

peach margarita
Follow the instructions for the Kiwi Margarita, substituting half a large, or
small, peeled, ripe peach for the kiwifruit.

variations

in the pink buck's fizz

see base recipe page 174

mr. mcgarry's buck's fizz
Prepare the basic receipe, but omit the Grenadine.

grapefruit fizz
Replace the orange juice with white or pink grapefruit juice and add the Grenadine or omit as preferred.

pineapple fizz
Replace the orange juice with pineapple juice and add the Grenadine or omit as preferred.

tropical fizz
Replace the orange juice with a tropical fruit juice such as mango, papaya, or watermelon.

frozen banana daiquiri

see base recipe page 177

frozen strawberry daiquiri
Prepare the basic recipe, substituting Crème de Fraise (strawberry liqueur) for
the Crème de Banane and 4–5 large strawberries, hulled and halved for the
banana. Decorate glasses with an extra whole strawberry instead of the lime
and banana slices.

frozen kiwi daiquiri
Prepare the basic recipe, substituting sweet Kiwifruit Liqueur for the Crème
de Banane and 1 peeled kiwifruit for the banana. Decorate glass with a
kiwifruit slice, instead of the lime and bananas.

frozen mango daiquiri
Prepare the basic recipe, substituting the chopped flesh of half a ripe mango
for the banana and mango liqueur for the Crème de Banane. Decorate glass
with just a lime slice or wedge.

minted berry daiquiri
Prepare the basic recipe, replacing the Crème de Banane with Crème de
Framboise (raspberry liqueur) and the banana with 1/2 cup frozen mixed
berries, such as strawberries, raspberries, blueberries, and blackberries.
Decorate glass with a mint sprig, instead of the lime and banana.

from the tropics

Just back from the vacation of a lifetime? Relive

those magic moments on a white beach by shaking

up a tropical storm. Whether it's a Piña Colada, Mai

Tai, Mojito, or "day-of-the-dead" Zombie, you'll be

holding a glass of paradise in your hand.

hurricane janet

see variations page 202

A hurricane might seem an unlikely cause for celebration, but the huge storm that hit the Caribbean island of Grenada in 1955 inspired this great party drink. A similar cocktail, with coconut added to the mix, hails from the same island and bears the name "Pain Killer."

1 1/2 fl. oz. gold rum
1 1/2 fl. oz. white rum
2 fl. oz. pineapple juice
4 fl. oz. orange juice
Juice of half a lime
Dash of Grenadine
Ice cubes
Slice of tropical fruit, to serve

Put the gold rum, white rum, pineapple juice, orange juice, lime juice, and Grenadine into a cocktail shaker. Shake well. Half-fill a highball glass or cocktail glass with ice cubes and strain in the drink. Serve with a straw and decorate with a slice of tropical fruit such as pineapple, mango, or papaya.

Serves 1

piña colada

see variations page 203

The first report of a drink called a piña colada can be traced back to the December 1922 edition of *Travel* magazine. Translated from Spanish, the name means "strained pineapple," and back then the cocktail was simply fresh pineapple juice, ice, sugar, lime juice, and white rum shaken together and strained into a glass. Ramon "Monchito" Marrero is one of several bartenders claiming the credit for adding coconut milk. A plaque in Puerto Rico states he served the first modern piña colada in the bar of the Caribe Hilton Hotel on August 15, 1954, after spending three months perfecting his mix.

1 fl. oz. white rum
2 fl. oz. thick coconut milk
4 fl. oz. pineapple juice
Crushed ice
Pineapple wedge, to serve

Put the white rum, coconut milk, and pineapple juice in a blender with 2–3 tablespoons of crushed ice. Blend until smooth. Pour into a cocktail glass and serve with a straw. Decorate the drink with a pineapple wedge.

Serves 1

mai tai

see variations page 204

In 1944, Victor Bergeron, better known throughout the restaurant world as "Trader Vic," sat down one evening with the bartender of his Polynesian restaurant in Oakland, California, and the two of them decided to invent a new drink. The resulting mix of Jamaican rum, lime juice, orgeat syrup, Orange Curacao, and rock candy was offered to customers. One who tried it immediately exclaimed "Mai Tai, Roa Ae!" — which, as any Tahitian-speaker can tell you, means "out of this world."

2 fl. oz. gold rum
1/2 fl. oz. Orange Curacao
Juice of 1 lime
2 tsp orgeat syrup (almond syrup)
1 tsp. Grenadine (optional)
Crushed ice
Wedges of lime and mint sprig, to serve

Put the rum, Orange Curacao, lime juice, almond syrup, and Grenadine into a cocktail shaker. Shake vigorously. Strain into a glass half-filled with crushed ice, and serve decorated with wedges of lime and a mint sprig. Add a stirrer and straw.

Serves 1

zombie

see variations page 205

Don Beach created the Zombie cocktail in 1934 at his Beachcomber restaurant in Hollywood after asking a hungover customer how he felt. His exotic brews became the stuff of legend, with regular clients no doubt providing inspiration for many of his cocktails, although whether the Missionary's Downfall (fresh pineapple, lime juice, mint, rum, and peach brandy) was among them is not recorded. The original Zombie was a mix of 11 different ingredients, including a shot of 151-proof rum that was floated on top. The recipe given here is a slightly simplified — and marginally less lethal — version.

1/2 fl. oz. dark rum
1/2 fl. oz. gold rum
1/2 fl. oz. white rum or Malibu coconut rum
3/4 fl. oz. apricot brandy
1/3 fl. oz. lime juice
2 fl. oz. pineapple juice
1 tsp. sugar syrup
Crushed ice or ice cubes
Twist of lime zest, to serve

Put all the ingredients (except the ice) into a cocktail shaker and shake vigorously. Pour into a glass half-filled with crushed ice or ice cubes and stir well. Decorate glass with a twist of lime zest.

Serves 1

planter's punch

see variations page 206

This generic name covers the wide variety of simple, but potent, rum-based punches served all over the West Indian islands. The rum is mixed with different fruit juices and sometimes given an extra kick with locally grown spices such as nutmeg or cayenne. The first reference to a Planter's Punch can be traced to a poem in the *New York Times* on August 8, 1908, extolling the virtues of a drink made with Old Jamaican rum that packed a serious punch.

2 tbsp. freshly squeezed lime juice
2 tbsp. sugar syrup
3 fl. oz. dark rum
Dash of Angostura bitters
Crushed ice
Pieces of fruit, to serve

Put the lime juice, sugar syrup, rum, and Angostura in a cocktail shaker with 2–3 tablespoons of crushed ice and shake hard. Pour, unstrained, into a glass and decorate with pieces of fruit threaded onto a cocktail stick. Serve with a straw.

Serves 1

tropical fruit batida

see variations page 207

Batida is a Brazilian cocktail that features the national drink, Cachaca, with sugar and various tropical fruits. Almost any mixture of fruit seems to work. The Cachaca can also be replaced with vodka or white rum.

1/4 mango, peeled and sliced
1/4 papaya, peeled, deseeded, and sliced
2 fl. oz. Cachaca
3 tbsp. crushed ice
Mineral water

Put the mango and papaya in a blender; add the Cachaca and crushed ice; and blend until smooth. Pour into a cocktail glass and top off with sparkling or still mineral water. Serve with a straw.

Serves 1

jamaican rum punch

see variations page 208

This is one is from Jamaica, where there are many mixes featuring the locally brewed rum — all designed to seduce visitors as well as locals looking to chill out as the sun goes down.

Juice of 2 limes
1 fl. oz. orange juice
1 fl. oz. pineapple juice
2 tbsp. Grenadine syrup
2 fl. oz. light rum
Ice cubes or crushed ice
Orange, lime, and pineapple slices, to serve

Put the lime juice, orange juice, pineapple juice, Grenadine, rum, and plenty of ice, in a cocktail shaker. Shake vigorously. Strain into a glass and serve decorated with orange, lime, and pineapple slices.

Serves 1

mojito

see variations page 209

Along with cigars, the Mojito is one of Cuba's most famous exports. Its name (pronounced mo-hee-toe) comes from the African word "mojo," meaning to cast a little spell. Ernest Hemingway was known to down the odd Mojito in Havana's La Bodeguita del Medio bar, and James Bond followed his lead in *Die Another Day*.

4 mint leaves or 2 sprigs, plus extra to serve
1 tsp. superfine sugar or sugar syrup
Freshly squeezed juice of 1 lime
2 fl. oz. white rum
Ice cubes
Soda water
Lime wedge and star fruit slice, to serve

Put the mint leaves or sprigs, superfine sugar or sugar syrup, and lime juice in a mixing jug or straight into a tall glass. Muddle until the sugar dissolves and the oils are released from the mint, making it aromatic. Fill a glass with ice cubes, add the rum, and stir well. If using a mixing jug, strain or pour the mix into the glass, and top off with soda water. Serve decorated with a lime wedge, slice of star fruit, and an extra sprig of mint.

Serves 1

variations

hurricane janet

see base recipe page 189

tropical storm
Instead of gold and white rum, use all gold rum or a mix of gold and dark rum. Omit the orange juice and add 4 fl. oz. of pineapple juice.

force 8 gale
Blend the ingredients together in a blender with 2–3 tablespoons of crushed ice. Pour into a chilled glass.

calm after the storm
For a less alcoholic drink, reduce the quantity of rum by half and increase the quantity of pineapple juice by 1 1/2 fl. oz.

rough seas
Replace the Grenadine with a dash of Blue Curacao.

pain killer
Omit the Grenadine and add 1 fl. oz. coconut milk. Serve with a light sprinkling of freshly grated nutmeg.

piña colada

see base recipe page 190

malibu colada
For an extra kick, add 1 fl. oz. of Malibu coconut rum to the blender with the other ingredients.

chi chi
Substitute vodka — plain or vanilla — for the white rum.

amaretto piña colada
Add 3/4 fl. oz. Amaretto Disaronno to the blender with the other ingredients.

colada sundowner
For a more aromatic drink, use dark rum instead of white.

mango colada
Add the peeled, chopped flesh of half a ripe mango to the blender with the other ingredients. Increase the quantity of pineapple juice to 1 cup (8 fl. oz.) or a little more if the drink is too thick.

variations

mai tai

see base recipe page 193

long, tall mai tai
Strain the mix into a well-chilled highball glass over 4 or 5 ice cubes and top off with pineapple juice.

apricot mai tai
Add 1/2 fl. oz. apricot brandy to the cocktail shaker with the other ingredients.

orange mai tai
Add 1 fl. oz. orange juice to the mix in the shaker, or pour the mix over ice into a tall glass and top off with orange juice.

mango mai tai
Add 1 tablespoon of mango nectar to the cocktail shaker with the other ingredients and omit the Grenadine.

vodka mai tai
Replace the gold rum with vodka and add 1 fl. oz. orange juice to the mix.

variations

zombie

see base recipe page 194

orange zombie
Reduce the lime juice to just a squeeze, increase the quantity of pineapple juice to 3 fl. oz., and add the same amount of freshly squeezed orange juice.

cherry & almond zombie
Replace the apricot brandy with cherry brandy and the sugar syrup with almond syrup.

beginner's zombie
Too many Zombies can indeed turn you into the walking dead, so for a less punishing cocktail, cut the total quantity of rum in half — use just white or gold — and triple the quantity of pineapple juice or replace it with orange juice.

dead man's chest zombie
Seriously crazy revelers can add over-proof rum instead of the gold rum, but don't say you haven't been warned.

south sea island zombie
Replace the pineapple juice with papaya juice and add a mixture of chopped tropical fruits, such as mangos, papaya, pineapple, and banana to the glass.

variations

planter's punch

see base recipe page 196

knock-out punch
Serve the punch dusted with fiery cayenne pepper or freshly grated nutmeg.

long, cool punch
Reduce the quantity of rum by half. Serve the punch in a tall glass topped with soda water.

puerto rican planter's punch
Halve the quantity of dark rum, shake with the other ingredients (omitting the crushed ice) and pour unstrained into a tall glass. Add ice cubes, a splash of soda water, and float 1–2 tablespoons of 151 proof rum on top.

orange planter's punch
Instead of making the basic recipe, shake 2 fl. oz. dark rum in a cocktail shaker with 1 teaspoon of lime juice and 2 fl. oz orange juice. Strain into a glass filled with ice cubes and serve with a stirrer.

white planter's punch
Instead of making the basic recipe, pour 1 tablespoon of sugar syrup and 2 fl. oz. of white rum into a glass. Add a strip of lime zest, twisting it as you drop it in to release the citrus oil. Add ice cubes and top off with still or sparkling water to taste.

tropical fruit batida

see base recipe page 197

watermelon batida
Replace the mango and papaya with a small, peeled, deseeded wedge of watermelon.

guava & lychee batida
Replace the mango and papaya with one peeled, deseeded guava and two peeled, pitted lychees (or two canned lychees, drained).

kiwi batida
Replace the mango and papaya with 1 peeled, chopped kiwifruit.

strawberry batida
Replace the mango and papaya with 4–5 hulled, ripe strawberries (depending on size).

papaya vodka batida
Omit the mango and double the amount of papaya. Replace the Cachaca with the same amount of vodka. Add the juice of half a lime and 2 teaspoons sugar syrup. Blend all the ingredients with the crushed ice until smooth. Pour into a glass and top off with mineral water.

variations

jamaican rum punch

see base recipe page 198

the gleaner
Pour 2 fl. oz. Jamaican rum into a glass half-filled with crushed ice,
1 teaspoon sugar syrup, and a slice of pineapple and orange.

trinidadian rum punch
Shake together 3 fl. oz. dark rum, with one tablespoon Grenadine,
1 teaspoon sugar syrup, and the juice of one lime and half a lemon.
Strain over ice into a glass.

antiguan rum punch
Shake together 3 fl. oz. white rum, the juice of 1 lime, and 1 tablespoon
sugar syrup. Strain over ice into a tall glass and top off with soda water.

grenadan rum punch
Shake together 3 fl. oz. dark rum, 1 1/2 fl. oz. lemon juice, and 2 tablespoons
Grenadine. Pour over ice into a tall glass and top off with soda water.

bajan rum punch
Put the lime juice in a pitcher with two tablespoons of sugar syrup, 3 fl. oz.
Bajan rum, and 4 fl. oz. still mineral water. Stir well. Pour into a tall glass
filled with ice and add a dash of Angostura and a sprinkling of freshly
grated nutmeg.

mojito

see base recipe page 201

lychee & raspberry mojito
Muddle 1 peeled, pitted, chopped fresh lychee (or 1 canned lychee, drained) and 4 raspberries with the mint, sugar, and lime juice, but do this in the glass rather than a jug so the fruit can be enjoyed with the drink.

strawberry & black pepper mojito
Make the Lychee Mojito, but use 2–3 chopped, hulled strawberries, and 2 grindings of black pepper.

mango mojito
Make the Lychee Mojito, but muddle 1 tablespoon of chopped ripe mango flesh in the glass with the mint, sugar, and lime juice.

blackberry mojito
Make the Lychee Mojito, but muddle 5 blackberries in the glass with the mint, sugar, and lime juice.

mojito royale
Muddle the mint, sugar, and lime juice in a cocktail shaker, add half the rum, and shake well. Strain into a champagne flute, top off with well-chilled champagne, and serve decorated with a sprig of mint.

after-dinner drinks & winter warmers

Keep the long winter nights at bay with a reviving

mug of Mulled Wine or Spiced Apple Toddy, and

round off a relaxing supper with a warming

glass of Gaelic Coffee, Real Hot Chocolate, or a

conversation-stopping Pousse Café. Each one is

guaranteed to banish the winter blues.

spiced hot toddy

see variations page 224

If you're feeling under the weather, this should have you back to your old self in no time. Use a clear honey and stir it into the other ingredients over a low heat until it dissolves.

1/4 pt. apple juice
1 fl. oz. Apple Schnapps
1 tsp. honey
1 star anise
Apple slices, to serve

Put the apple juice, Apple Schnapps, honey, and star anise in a small pan. Warm through gently without boiling, stirring until the honey dissolves. Cool for 1 minute and then pour into a glass. Serve with a couple of apple slices dropped into the drink.

Serves 1

gaelic coffee

see variations page 225

What better way is there to round off a winter meal than to sit back and sip a glass of Gaelic coffee, savoring every mouthful as you slowly drink the hot coffee through the head of rich, luscious cream. Two tips for making sure the cream floats — the coffee and whiskey mixture must be sweetened and the cream must be poured very slowly over the back of a spoon so it skims the surface and doesn't plop into the coffee.

1 fl. oz. Irish whiskey
1 tsp. soft brown sugar
4 fl. oz. hot strong black coffee
About 2 fl. oz. chilled heavy cream

Warm a goblet or cocktail glass. Add the whiskey and sugar and pour in the hot coffee, stirring until the sugar dissolves. Slowly pour the cream over the back of a spoon into the glass and allow it to stand for a few minutes to give the cream time to float on the surface before serving.

Serves 1

mulled wine

see variations page 226

Not a drink to make just for yourself, but one that's guaranteed to ensure a warm welcome for Christmas carolers or New Year party guests. Overheating will cause too much of the alcohol to evaporate, so allow the mix to just come to a simmer. Once made, the best way to keep the mulled wine warm is in a slow cooker where it will stay hot but not boil.

1 cup (8 fl. oz.) water
2/3 cup superfine sugar
2 small oranges or 3 clementines, studded with
    4 or 5 whole cloves
1 lemon, sliced
2 cinnamon sticks
1 bottle dry red table wine
1/2 bottle ruby port
Freshly grated nutmeg, to serve

Put the water in a large suacepan. Add the sugar, oranges or clementines, and lemon slices. Heat gently until the sugar dissolves, then add the cinnamon sticks, wine, and port, and heat until simmering. Remove from the heat and serve very hot with a nutmeg grated on top.

Serves 12

real hot chocolate

see variations page 227

It's worth buying good quality chocolate with around 70% cocoa solids to turn this nursery bedtime drink into a rich, satisfying grown-up treat. Sip the chocolate through the whipped cream, or stir it in and let it dissolve, as you prefer.

2 oz. dark chocolate, chopped
7 fl. oz. milk
1 fl. oz. white Crème de Cacao
Sugar or sugar syrup, to taste
Whipped cream, to serve
Grated chocolate, to serve

Put the chocolate in a double boiler to melt or in the microwave. Stir until smooth. Heat the milk until it comes to a boil, pour a little into the chocolate, and whisk until mixed. Gradually blend in the rest of the milk, stir in the Crème de Cacao, and pour into a heavy glass or mug. Taste and sweeten with a little sugar or sugar syrup if necessary. Top with whipped cream and grated chocolate.

Serves 1

brandy alexander

see variations page 228

A gin-based cocktail called simply "Alexander" was popular during the early part of the twentieth century. The Brandy Alexander was reputedly created in 1922, as an after-dinner drink to celebrate the London wedding of the Princess Royal to the British aristocrat Viscount Lascelles.

1 fl. oz. brown Crème de Cacao
1 fl. oz. double cream
1 fl. oz. brandy
Ice cubes
Grated nutmeg, to serve

Pour Crème de Cacao and cream into a cocktail shaker, add the brandy and plenty of ice cubes, and shake vigorously. Strain into a brandy glass and top with a little grated nutmeg.

Serves 1

night owl

see variations page 229

Coffee, orange, and cream make an irresistible after-dinner drink, especially during the cold winter months when you're curled up in a soft, deep armchair beside a blazing fire. The three ingredients can be shaken together or the cream can be floated on top.

1 fl. oz. Tia Maria or Kahlúa
1 fl. oz. Triple Sec
1 fl. oz. light cream
Ice cubes (optional)

Put the Tia Maria, Triple Sec, and cream into a cocktail shaker with or without some ice cubes. Shake vigorously. Strain into a small glass and serve immediately.

Serves 1

pousse café

see variations page 230

Layered cocktails not only look impressive but they make very good after-dinner drinks. Each liquor has a different density, so as long as the heaviest liquid is poured into the glass first, followed by the second heaviest, the third heaviest, and so on, finishing with the lightest, the individual liquids will remain separate, producing a rainbow-layered drink. In general terms, syrups and sweet drinks are the heaviest, flavored liqueurs are in the middle, and spirits are the lightest, but you may need to experiment first, as the densities of individual liquors can vary from one manufacturer to another.

1/3 fl. oz. Grenadine
1/3 fl. oz. green Crème de Menthe
1/3 fl. oz. Blue Curacao
1/3 fl. oz. Benedictine
1/3 fl. oz. brandy

Layer the ingredients into a shot or sherry glass in the order listed above. Pour the Grenadine into the glass. For subsequent layers, pour each liquid into a small pitcher first and then drizzle it very slowly over the back of a spoon, so it floats on the layer below. Give the layers a few moments to settle before serving. The drink can be make in advance and chilled in the refrigerator until needed.

Serves 1

rusty nail

see variations page 231

Drambuie is a Scottish liqueur of Scotch whiskey flavored with honey, so it's no surprise that its Gaelic name translates as "the drink that satisfies." Serve this over ice or straight up, as you prefer.

2 fl. oz. Scotch whiskey
1 fl. oz. Drambuie
Twist of lemon, to serve

Pour the Scotch into a tumbler over ice or not, as preferred. Add the Drambuie and stir well. Drop in a twist of lemon and serve.

Serves 1

variations

spiced hot toddy

see base recipe page 211

spiced orange toddy
Replace the apple juice with orange juice and the Apple Schnapps with
Cointreau. Serve with an orange slice instead of apple slices.

spiced cranberry peach toddy
Replace the apple juice with cranberry juice and the Apple Schnapps with
Peach Schnapps. Serve with a couple of peaches instead of apple slices.

spiced grapefruit toddy
Replace the apple juice with grapefruit juice and the Apple Schnapps
with plain or grapefruit-flavored vodka. Serve with a couple of grapefruit
segments instead of apple slices.

spiced pineapple toddy
Replace the apple juice with pineapple juice and the Apple Schnapps with
gold rum. Serve with a wedge of pineapple instead of apple slices.

spiced cherry toddy
Replace the Apple Schnapps with cherry brandy or kirsch. Serve with a
maraschino cherry on a cocktail stick instead of apple slices.

variations

gaelic coffee

see base recipe page 212

calypso coffee
Replace the Irish whiskey with Tia Maria.

normandy coffee
Replace the Irish whiskey with Calvados.

italian coffee completo
Replace the Irish whiskey with Grappa.

tokyo coffee
Replace the Irish whiskey with sake.

russian coffee
Replace the Irish whiskey with vodka.

variations

mulled wine

see base recipe page 215

gluhwein
Replace port with red wine and add 1 cup (8 fl. oz.) orange juice instead of
oranges or clementines. Add 3 cloves and 6 allspice berries, 1 split vanilla
pod, and the cinnamon sticks. Serve with raisins instead of nutmeg.

julglogg
Make as for Gluhwein, omitting the orange juice and replacing it with gin.

the bishop
Put the oranges or clementines in a pan. Add 1 1/2 bottles ruby port, 2 cups
water, and 2 oz. superfine sugar. Add cinnamon sticks and simmer.

mulled rum punch
Place 1 cup water in pan with 7 oz. brown sugar, rind of 2 oranges, and
1 lemon. Boil until reduced by half. Place in another pan, add the juice of 2
oranges and lemon, cinnamon sticks, and 1/2 pint dark rum. Simmer.

mulled ale
Place lemon rind and juice in a saucepan. Add 1 cup (8 fl. oz.) light ale,
4 tablespoons brandy, 4 tablespoons dark rum, 1/2 cup water, 2 tablespoons
demerera sugar, and 2 cinnamon sticks. Heat until almost boiling and serve.

variations

real hot chocolate

see base recipe page 216

minty hot chocolate
Replace the white Crème de Cacao with white Crème de Menthe and serve
with grated mint chocolate on top.

orange hot chocolate
Replace the white Crème de Cacao with Cointreau and serve with grated
orange chocolate on top.

brandied hot chocolate
Replace the white Crème de Cacao with brandy.

mocha chocolate
Replace the white Crème de Cacao with Kahlúa or Tia Maria.

coconut hot chocolate
Replace the white Crème de Cacao with Malibu Coconut Rum and serve
with toasted dried, shredded coconut sprinkled on top.

variations

brandy alexander

see base recipe page 218

choc-topped brandy alexander
Serve the drink in a wide-brimmed, shallow cocktail glass such as a saucer-shaped champagne glass. Before pouring in the drink, rub the rim of the glass with a lemon wedge and dip it in grated dark chocolate.

white brandy alexander
Replace the dark Crème de Cacao with white Crème de Cacao.

brandy alexander frozen smoothie
Put the Crème de Cacao and brandy in a blender and add 1/2 cup (4 fl. oz.) vanilla ice cream. Blend until creamy and smooth then pour into a   brandy glass.

amaretto alexander
Replace the brandy with Amaretto Disaronno and double the quantity of cream.

apricot alexander
Replace the brandy with apricot brandy.

variations

night owl

see base recipe page 219

owl with a night cap
Pour the Tia Maria and Triple Sec into a small glass. Replace the light cream with heavy cream and carefully float it on top of the drink.

long cool night owl
Shake the ingredients together without any ice. Pour mix over ice into a tumbler. Serve with a stirrer.

amaretto night owl
Replace the Triple Sec with Amaretto Disaronno.

spirit of the night
Replace the Triple Sec with mandarin- or orange-flavored vodka.

mocha night owl
Replace the Triple Sec with white or brown Crème de Cacao.

variations

pousse café

see base recipe page 221

independence day
For a Fourth of July or Bastille Day party, layer Grenadine, followed by white Crème de Menthe, and then Blue Curacao.

you've passed!
Celebrate passing your driving test with a "traffic light" layering of Grenadine, followed by Galliano, and then melon liqueur.

coffee, peaches & cream
For a sultry summer evening, layer ice-cold Kahlúa, peach schnapps, and Bailey's Irish Cream liqueur.

bellissimo
Round off an Italian meal with a liquid tricolor — Grenadine, followed by Amaretto Disaronno, and green Chartreuse.

give thanks
Celebrate Thanksgiving by layering Peach Schnapps, followed by cranberry juice, and finally vodka.

rusty nail

see base recipe page 222

vodka rusty nail
Replace the whiskey with the same quantity of vodka.

auld nick
Shake half quantities of the Scotch and Drambuie with 1 tablespoon each of orange and lemon juice. Strain into a tumbler over ice and decorate with a lemon twist.

isle of skye
Shake together 1 fl. oz. Drambuie, 1 fl. oz. gin, and 1 fl. oz. lemon juice. Serve straight up or over ice garnished with a lemon twist.

rob roy
Stir or shake together the Scotch with 1/2 fl. oz. dry white vermouth, a dash of Angostura bitters, and half a teaspoon of syrup from a jar of maraschino cherries. Serve strained, into a well-chilled cocktail glass, decorated with a cherry.

malted martini
Shake or stir together 2 fl. oz. vodka with 1/2 fl. oz. single malt (the smoky malts from Islay work well). Strain into a glass. Serve with an olive on a cocktail stick.

virgin cocktails

Don't drink and drive — you know it makes sense — but when it's your turn to chauffeur your fellow revelers home, you needn't miss out on all the fun. These nonalcoholic indulgences taste as good as they look and will make any occasion go with a swing.

pussyfoot

see variations page 248

A virgin cocktail dating from the 1920s and the years of Prohibition, it was named for William E. "Pussyfoot" Johnson, an anti-liquor campaigner who fought fiercely to convince his fellow men of the evils of liquor. Things weren't all they seemed, however; in 1926 the same Mr. Johnson was forced to admit that, in the pursuit of his cause, he had had to drink "gallons of alcohol" to give him strength to keep going.

1 fl. oz. orange juice
1 fl. oz. lime juice
1 fl. oz. lemon juice
Dash of Grenadine
1 fresh egg yolk (from a free-range egg)
Ice cubes
Twist of lime zest, to serve

Pour the orange juice, lime juice, lemon juice, Grenadine, and egg yolk into a cocktail shaker with plenty of ice cubes. Shake hard. Strain into a wine glass and serve with a twist of lime zest.

Serves 1

ice bite

see variations page 249

More than a hint of pink makes this long, tall cooler just right for a summer's day. If making it for a picnic, put the ingredients into a thermos with the ice and shake well before serving.

2 fl. oz. pink grapefruit juice
4 fl. oz. cranberry juice
Juice of 1/2 lime
Crushed ice

Put the grapefruit juice, cranberry juice, and lime juice into a cocktail shaker. Shake well. Fill a tall glass with crushed ice and pour in the drink.

Serves 1

lime, mint & lemongrass sparkler

see variations page 250

Fragrant mint combined with exotic lemongrass and sparkling apple juice makes a delicious, long, and cooling beverage.

4 sprigs of fresh mint
1/2 lemongrass stalk, tough outer leaves
    removed, finely chopped
1 tbsp. Rose's Lime Juice (or mix equal
    quantities sugar syrup and fresh lime juice)
Ice cubes
Sparkling apple juice
Apple slices and lime wedge, to serve

Put the mint and lemongrass into a tall glass with the lime juice and muddle together to release their flavors. Half-fill the glass with ice and top off with sparkling apple juice. Serve decorated with apple slices and a lime wedge.

Serves 1

piña moclada

see variations page 251

Cool, creamy, and refreshing, serve this virgin cousin of the Piña Colada in a tall glass with plenty of ice.

1/2 banana, peeled and chopped
7 fl. oz. pineapple juice
3 fl. oz. coconut milk
Ice

Put the banana, pineapple juice, and coconut milk in a blender. Blend until smooth and creamy. Pour into a tall glass half-filled with ice and serve with a straw.

Serves 1

kiwi crush

see variations page 252

Served in a cocktail glass with a frosted sugar rim this will bring a smile to the face of teens desperate to emulate their older siblings and drivers wanting to get into the party spirit without the alcohol.

Lime wedge
Superfine sugar
1 tbsp. freshly squeezed lime juice
1/2 tsp. sugar syrup, or to taste
1 kiwifruit, peeled and chopped
2 fl. oz. apple juice

Rub the rim of a cocktail glass with the lime wedge, and dip in the superfine sugar to coat in an even layer. Put the lime juice, sugar syrup, chopped kiwifruit, and the apple juice in a blender. Blend until smooth. Pour into a martini glass and serve at once.

Serves 1

shirley temple

see variations page 253

Probably the first virgin "mocktail" was named in honor of the 1930s child film star. It makes the perfect drink for pretty girls everywhere. The ginger ale adds a nice spicy edge to the sweet and long drink.

Ice cubes
2 dashes of Grenadine
3/4–1 cup (6–8 fl. oz.) ginger ale
Lemon wedges, to serve

Fill a tall highball glass with ice. Add a couple of dashes of Grenadine and top off with the ginger ale. Squeeze a couple of lemon wedges over the top before droping them in the drink. Stir and serve.

Serves 1

red berry soda

see variations page 254

A good summer party drink when homegrown strawberries are at their best. Although strawberries lose their texture when frozen, it doesn't matter as they are puréed for this drink. If you have extra strawberries freeze them to use later in the year.

1 tsp. raspberry syrup or plain sugar syrup
2/3 cup sliced strawberries
2 fl. oz. raspberry juice
Ice cubes
1/2 cup (4 fl. oz.) soda water
Raspberries and extra strawberries, to serve

Put the raspberry syrup, strawberries, and raspberry juice in a blender. Blend until smooth. Pour into a highball glass half-filled with ice cubes and top off with the soda water. Serve decorated with raspberries and extra strawberries.

Serves 1

mango & coconut refresher

see variations page 255

Another taste of the sun-kissed Caribbean, courtesy of this smooth, creamy cooler. Use a very ripe, sweet, and fragrant mango so the finished drink has plenty of fresh, fruity flavor.

1/2 ripe mango, peeled and chopped
2 fl. oz. thick coconut milk
Ice cubes
About 1/2 cup (4 fl. oz.) soda water

Put the mango and coconut milk in a blender, and blend until smooth. Pour into a tall glass half-filled with ice cubes and top off with soda water.

Serves 1

variations

pussyfoot

see base recipe page 233

pussyfoot frappe
Put all the ingredients except the ice cubes into a blender. Add 2–3 tablespoons of crushed ice and blend together until the ice is finely crushed. Pour into a large wine glass and serve with a straw.

orange pussyfoot
Double the quantity of orange juice and reduce by half the amount of both the lime juice and lemon juice.

grapefruit pussyfoot
Replace the lime juice and lemon juice with 2 fl. oz. white grapefruit juice.

apple pussyfoot
Replace the lime juice and lemon juice with 2 fl. oz. apple juice.

strawberry pussyfoot
Replace the Grenadine with 1 teaspoon strawberry syrup.

variations

ice bite

see base recipe page 234

orange ice bite
Replace the pink grapefruit juice with the same quantity of orange juice.

apple ice bite
Replace the pink grapefruit juice with the same quantity of apple juice.

goji berry ice bite
Replace the pink grapefruit juice with goji berry juice.

pineapple ice bite
Replace the pink grapefruit juice with white grapefruit juice and the cranberry juice with pineapple juice.

pink cloud ice bite
Replace the cranberry juice with blood orange juice.

lime, mint & lemongrass sparkler

see base recipe page 237

lemon & mint sparkler
Replace the lime with a wedge of lemon, and muddle it with the mint and lemongrass. Add ice and top off with lemonade or bitter lemon instead of apple juice. Serve decorated with a lemon slice.

st. clements sparkler
Replace the sparkling apple juice with a sparkling orange drink. Decorate the glass with just the lime wedge.

mint & cola sparkler
Omit the lime and replace the sparkling apple juice with cola. Omit the apple slices and lime wedge.

mint & ginger sparkler
Omit the lime and replace the sparkling apple juice with ginger ale. Omit the apple slices and lime wedge.

mint & strawberry sparkler
Replace the lemongrass with 2 chopped strawberries and the lime with 1 teaspoon strawberry syrup. Top off with sparkling mineral water. Decorate the glass with a mint sprig.

variations

piña moclada

see base recipe page 238

sunrise moclada
Add a dash of Grenadine to the finished drink and stir before drinking.

mango moclada
Replace the banana with the chopped, peeled flesh of half a ripe mango.

strawberry moclada
Replace the banana with 4 large, hulled strawberries and add a dash of strawberry syrup.

kiwi moclada
Replace the banana with 1 peeled and chopped kiwifruit, and replace half the pineapple juice with apple juice.

papaya moclada
Replace the banana with the chopped, peeled, and deseeded flesh of half a small ripe papaya.

variations

kiwi crush

see base recipe page 241

strawberry crush
Replace the kiwifruit with 4 hulled strawberries, and use strawberry syrup
instead of plain sugar syrup.

mango crush
Replace the kiwifruit with the chopped flesh of half a ripe mango.

clementine crush
Replace the kiwifruit with a peeled clementine. After blending the
ingredients, strain the mixture into the glass.

apricot crush
Replace the kiwifruit with 2 pitted apricots, adding a little more apple juice
if the drink is too thick.

peach crush
Replace the kiwifruit with the chopped flesh of half a ripe peach. After
blending the ingredients, strain the mixture into the glass. Add a little more
apple juice if the drink is too thick.

variations

shirley temple

see base recipe page 242

strawberry shirley temple
Replace the Grenadine with strawberry syrup.

raspberry shirley temple
Replace the Grenadine with raspberry syrup, and the ginger ale with bitter lemon.

lemon drop kid
Replace the ginger ale with lemonade or 7-Up.

orange drop kid
Replace the ginger ale with a sparkling orange drink.

roy rogers
We can't let the boys feel left out! Replace the ginger ale with cola.

variations

red berry soda

see base recipe page 245

raspberry & blueberry soda
Purée the syrup with 1/2 cup blueberries instead of strawberries and serve decorated with raspberries and extra blueberries.

strawberry & elderflower soda
Purée the strawberries with 1 tablespoon elderflower juice instead of syrup.

red berry & apple soda
Top off with sparkling apple juice instead of soda water.

red berry & lemon soda
Top off with lemonade or bitter lemon instead of soda water.

blackberry soda
Purée the syrup with 1/2 cup blackberries instead of strawberries and serve decorated with raspberries and extra blackberries.

mango & coconut refresher

see base recipe page 246

mango, coconut & apple refresher
Top off with sparkling apple juice rather than soda water.

papaya & coconut refresher
Replace the mango with the chopped, peeled, deseeded flesh of half a small ripe papaya.

lychee & coconut refresher
Replace the mango with 4 peeled, pitted, canned rambutans if available, or substitute lychees.

watermelon & coconut refresher
Replace the mango with the chopped flesh of a small wedge of peeled, deseeded watermelon.

raspberry & coconut refresher
Replace the mango with 8 fresh or frozen raspberries.

hangover cures

If you're suffering the after-effects of last night's celebrations, one of these hangover cures should set you back on the straight and narrow. Be warned, though, they're too good to be filed away under "hair of the dog," and you'll find all sorts of excuses for mixing one up.

walk the line

see variations page 273

Ginger is well-known for settling a stomach with a mind of its own, so this long, spicy refresher should have you back on your feet and ready to rock 'n' roll all over again.

2 fl. oz. vodka
Juice of 1 lime
Dash of sugar syrup
Ice cubes
1/2 cup (4 fl. oz.) well-chilled ginger ale
Lime wedges, to serve

Put the vodka, lime juice, sugar syrup, and plenty of ice cubes into a cocktail shaker. Shake vigorously. Strain into a glass and top off with well-chilled ginger ale. Serve with lime wedges.

Serves 1

bullshot

see variations page 274

If you can't face any of the appetizers on the lunch menu, this full-flavored cocktail would make a revitalizing alternative to soup. Chill the bouillon well before shaking it with the other ingredients.

2 fl. oz. vodka
1/2 cup (4 fl. oz.) chilled beef bouillon or
    well-flavored stock
Dash lemon juice
2–3 dashes Worcestershire sauce
Pinch of celery salt
1–2 dashes Tabasco
Twist of lime or lemon, to serve

Put the vodka, bouillon, lemon juice, Worcestershire sauce, celery salt, and Tabasco in a cocktail shaker. Add extra Worcestershire sauce or Tabasco if you want to spice the mix up. Shake well, strain into a tumbler, and add a twist of lime or lemon. Serve with a stirrer.

Serves 1

eggnog

see variations page 275

Originally a punch made with milk and wine or sherry, eggnog became a popular tipple in English taverns during the eighteenth century when it was served in small, carved, mugs known as noggins. The drink later became associated with Christmas, with many Victorians believing the celebrations hadn't properly begun until they'd downed a glass of eggnog — which no doubt helped cure the effects of over indulgence the night before. When the drink crossed the Atlantic to America, rum replaced the sherry and became so popular that even George Washington created his own recipe, which included rye whiskey, rum, and sherry.

1 large egg, separated
1 1/2 tsp. superfine sugar
Few drops of vanilla extract
2 fl. oz. dark, gold, or white rum
3 fl. oz. full-fat milk
2 fl. oz. heavy cream
Freshly grated nutmeg, to dust

Put the egg yolk, sugar, and vanilla in a bowl and whisk together until pale and creamy. Gradually whisk in the rum, followed by the milk. In a separate bowl, whisk the egg white until it stands in soft peaks. Fold the egg yolk mixture into the whisked white. Whip the cream until it just holds its shape and then fold it in as well. Spoon into a glass and serve dusted with a little freshly grated nutmeg.

Serves 1

fluffy duck

see variations page 276

If you're hungover, one look at this smooth, creamy treat should make you feel better right away. The smoothing effect of Advocaat, with its light almond flavor, mixed with orange juice, cream, lemonade, and a gentle kick of rum, is ideal for banishing those "morning after" blues.

1 fl. oz. white rum
1 fl. oz. advocaat
Crushed ice
1 fl. oz. cream
1 fl. oz. orange juice
About 4 fl. oz. lemonade

Pour the rum and Advocaat into a tall glass half-filled with crushed ice. Add the cream and orange juice, stir, and then top off with lemonade. Serve with a straw.

Serves 1

snowball

see variations page 277

Egg yolks, vanilla, brandy, and sugar make up the liqueur Advocaat — almost a breakfast in a bottle! In the 1960s when the Snowball cocktail was at the height of its popularity, the alcohol content was so low it was disparagingly written off as a drink for the girls. Since then more potent brews have appeared, and variations with added gin or vodka have all done their bit to give the feminine Snowball a more macho image.

2 fl. oz. Advocaat
3/4 fl. oz. lime juice
Ice cubes
About 1/2 cup (4 fl. oz.) lemonade
Maraschino cherry, to serve

Put the Advocaat and lime juice into a cocktail shaker with plenty of ice cubes. Shake vigorously. Then strain into a large wine glass. Or, pour the well-chilled Advocaat into the glass over the ice cubes, and stir in the lime juice. Top off with lemonade and serve decorated with a maraschino cherry on a cocktail stick.

Serves 1

wake-up call

see variations page 278

If you have an important appointment the morning after a heavy night, this will probably get you there in time to do business better than the most insistent alarm! A little grated chocolate sprinkled over the creamy coffee drink also proves that every little bit helps.

1 fl. oz. gold rum
1 fl. oz. Amaretto Disaronno
2 tbsp. heavy cream
1 fl. oz. cold strong black coffee or a shot of
    espresso
Ice cubes
Grated dark chocolate, to serve

Put the rum, Amaretto Disaronno, cream, and coffee into a cocktail shaker with plenty of ice cubes. Shake vigorously. Strain into a cocktail glass and grate a little dark chocolate on top.

Serves 1

red restorer

see variations page 279

Deflect attention from the red eyes with this bright and breezy morning-after brew. The long list of superfood hits found in pomegranates and cranberries means it's also doing you a lot of good!

1 fl. oz. pomegranate juice
1 fl. oz. cranberry juice
1 fl. oz. vodka
Crushed ice
2 tsp. pomegranate seeds

Put the pomegranate juice, cranberry juice, and vodka in a cocktail shaker. Shake vigorously. Pour into a glass over crushed ice and scatter pomegranate seeds on top.

Serves 1

tokyo bloody mary

see variations page 280

The traditional Bloody Mary hangover cure was created in 1921 at Harry's Bar in Paris, but the inspiration for its name was reputedly America's sweetheart, Mary Pickford, rather than the unfortunate Mary Queen of Scots. Although not even her critics implied the silent-movie star was in need of morning-after restoratives, she had previously drunk a similar cocktail, so the new drink was named after her — blood depicting the tomato juice rather than any reflection on the lady herself!

1/2 cup (4 fl. oz.) tomato juice
2 fl. oz. sake
1 tsp. mirin
1/2 tsp. wasabi paste
Dash of Japanese soy sauce
Ice cubes
Celery stick, to serve

Put the tomato juice, sake, mirin, wasabi paste, and soy sauce in a tall glass over ice. Stir until all the ingredients are combined. Or, shake together in a cocktail shaker, and then pour into the glass over the ice. Serve with a celery stick as a stirrer.

Serves 1

hair of the dog

see variations page 281

Honey is prized for its soothing qualities and combined with whiskey and heavy cream, it's a good way to shake off those hangover blues.

2 fl. oz. whiskey
1 1/2 fl. oz. heavy cream
1 tbsp. clear honey
Ice cubes or crushed ice

Put the whiskey, heavy cream, and honey into a bowl and whisk together until combined, or shake vigorously together in a cocktail shaker. Pour into a tumbler over ice and serve with a stirrer and straw.

Serves 1

variations

walk the line

see base recipe page 257

cola line
Cola is another reliable stomach-settler. Replace the ginger ale with the same quantity of cola.

lemon line
Replace the lime juice with 1 tablespoon lemon juice and top off with half ginger ale and half lemonade. Decorate with a lemon wedge instead of lime wedges.

bitter orange line
Replace 1/2 fl. oz. of the vodka with Orange Curacao. Decorate drink with a small wedge of orange instead of lime wedges.

flat line
Replace the ginger ale with freshly squeezed orange juice.

variations

bullshot

see base recipe page 258

red rag
Replace half the beef bouillon with tomato juice.

veggie bull
Replace half the beef bouillon with vegetable bouillon and add the same amount of V8 vegetable juice.

orange bullshot
Add 1 tablespoon freshly squeezed orange juice to the cocktail shaker and shake with the other ingredients.

virgin bullshot
Replace the vodka with extra bouillon or tomato juice. Serve with a little black pepper ground over the top.

variations

eggnog

see base recipe page 261

warm eggnog
In a small pan, whisk together the whole egg, sugar, vanilla, milk, and cream over a low heat until the mixture thickens slightly — enough to coat the back of a spoon. Take care not to let the mixture get too hot, because it will separate. Put some fresh fruit, such as chopped pineapple, pitted cherries, or orange, in a glass. Add the rum and the eggnog. Sprinkle with nutmeg and drink while still warm.

nashville nog
Replace the rum with bourbon.

vanilla vodka nog
Omit the vanilla extract and replace the rum with vanilla vodka.

dry orange nog
Replace the rum with brandy and add a dash of Orange Curacao.

variations

fluffy duck

see base recipe page 262

chocolate fluffy duck
Prepare the basic recipe, but replace the white rum with white Crème de Cacao, and omit the orange juice.

fluffy duck soda
Replace the white rum with dark rum, omit the cream and increase the quantity of orange juice to 2 fl. oz. Top off with soda, rather than lemonade.

orange fluffy duck
Instead of making the basic recipe, pour 1/2 fl. oz. gin and 1/2 fl. oz. Cointreau into a tall glass half-filled with crushed ice. Add 1 fl. oz. heavy cream and 2 fl. oz. orange juice. Stir well, then top off with about 1/2 cup (4 fl. oz.) soda water.

apple fluffy duck
Top off with still or sparkling apple juice rather than lemonade.

variations

snowball

see base recipe page 265

dutch courage
Top off with pineapple juice rather than lemonade.

warm and spicy snowball
Top off with ginger ale rather than lemonade.

dutch breakfast
Replace half the Advocaat with gin and the lime juice with lemon juice.
Top off with sparkling or still apple juice and sweeten with a little sugar
syrup if desired.

melting snowball
Replace half the Advocaat with vodka. Pour the Advocaat, vodka, and lime
juice into a glass half-filled with crushed ice. Top off with lemonade.

variations

wake-up call

see base recipe page 266

espresso wake-up
Replace the gold rum with dark rum and double the amount of coffee.

white night wake-up
Replace the rum with vodka and the Amaretto Disaronno with white Crème de Cacao. Serve with a little white chocolate grated on top.

dead of night
Replace the rum with vanilla vodka and the Amaretto Disaronno with brown Crème de Cacao.

early riser
Replace the rum and Amaretto Disaronno with tequila.

variations

red restorer

see base recipe page 269

nervous breakdown
Replace the vodka with white rum and add a dash of Angostura instead of
pomegranate seeds. Serve decorated with a twist of lime.

headbanger
Stir the pomegranate and cranberry juices with sparkling vodka for a mildly
citrusy tingle on the tongue. Pour over crushed ice and decorate with a
small lemon slice instead of pomegranate seeds.

orange restorer
Replace the pomegranate juice with orange juice or blood orange juice.
Decorate with a small orange slice instead of pomegranate seeds.

double vision
Replace the pomegranate juice with lychee or mangosteen juice. Shake
with the other ingredients and pour into a glass over crushed ice. Omit the
pomegranate seeds.

variations

tokyo bloody mary

see base recipe page 270

bangkok bloody mary
Replace the sake with lemongrass-infused vodka, the mirin with sugar syrup, the wasabi paste with hot chili sauce, and the soy sauce with Thai fish sauce. Shake all the ingredients together, pour into a tall glass over ice, and garnish with a thin twist of lemon or lime zest.

traditional bloody mary
Stir or shake together the tomato juice with the juice of half a lemon, 2–3 dashes each of Worcestershire sauce and Tabasco, or 1/2 teaspoon prepared horseradish; 2 fl. oz. vodka, and a couple of grindings of black pepper. Pour into a tall glass over ice and sprinkle with a pinch of celery salt.

acapulco bloody mary
Make as for the traditional Bloody Mary, replacing the plain vodka with chili-infused vodka or tequila. Sprinkle a little deseeded and very finely chopped jalapeño pepper on top.

montmartre bloody mary
Make the traditional Bloody Mary replacing the vodka with Absinthe (an aniseed-flavored spirit with medicinal flowers and herbs).

variations

hair of the dog

see base recipe page 272

shaggy dog
Replace the cream with 1 fl. oz. Cointreau and 1/2 fl. oz. crème de banane.
Serve in a tall glass topped up with soda.

doggone
Replace the whiskey with brandy.

walkies
Replace the whiskey with 1/2 fl. oz. vanilla vodka and 1 1/2 fl. oz.
plain vodka.

dog day
Replace the whiskey with dark or gold rum.

index